'S.H. Came to Birmingham to school
of ' The Stockbroker clerk'.

SHERLOCK HOLMES

in the Midlands

anostic with B.han Germcdom of The adventure of
the Three garridebs. p54
A C D Knighted 1902

by Paul Lester

ACD left Dr Hoare's Aston practice in 1881

Dr watson's wife : Mary Morstan

Holme's fictional occupancy of 221B Baker St
was from 1880 to 1903. At the time there
was No 221 Baker St.

BREWIN BOOKS

First published
by Brewin Books, Studley, Warwickshire, B80 7LG
in September 1992

ISBN 0 947731 85 7

British Library Cataloguing in Publication Data.
A Catalogue record for this book is available from the British Library

Typeset in Plantin by Avon Dataset, Bidford on Avon, Warwickshire, B50 4JH
and made and printed by The Cromwell Press, Broughton Gifford, Melksham, Wiltshire.

Contents

Map of Midland counties of England c. 1890
indicating places of relevance.

Introduction

To readers of the Sherlock Holmes stories Baker Street in London is the location forever associated with the legendary detective. But the Midlands counties of England, perhaps most especially the area of Birmingham, have a claim to important associations with the detective and his creator, and made a significant contribution to the shaping of both, which it is to be hoped this work will go some way towards acknowledging.

The book's opening chapters bring together the early connections that the author of the Sherlock Holmes stories, Arthur Conan Doyle, had with the Midlands, namely the formative times he worked as a medical assistant in Ruyton and in Aston. These spells marked the beginning of Conan Doyle's short, and none too lucrative career as a medical man. Much more saliently, they marked too the inception of his long and immensely lucrative career as a writer. Investigation of these periods provide a number of intriguing clues to the inspiration for Conan Doyle's best known work, which concerns his detective hero Sherlock Holmes.

A chapter deals with Conan Doyle's associations with Staffordshire, in particular when cast in the role of a real life amateur sleuth, and there is a chapter on his connections with Midlands men in the spiritualist movement, which also had elements of the self-styled amateur detective at work. These two chapters offer some curious sidelights on the creator of Sherlock Holmes and upon the suspicion, which has sometimes been entertained, that Conan Doyle could in some way be identified with his detective creation.

Our attention then turns to examining the adventures of Sherlock Holmes in the Midlands counties. Though there is some investigation of a number of other minor references to the area found in the tales, which range in subject matter from prize-fighting to bicycling and deadly diseases, principally here the concern is with the three adventures which take our detective to Herefordshire in 'The Boscombe Valley Mystery', to

1

Introduction

Derbyshire in 'The Adventure of the Priory School' and to Birmingham in 'The Adventure of the Stockbroker's Clerk'. These tales reveal, apart from much else, the use the author made of his knowledge of Midlands history, geography and characters.

Finally the book records some of the other enduring indications of the link of Sherlock Holmes with the Midlands which might otherwise be overlooked, including a couple of minor mysteries which could well have made some passing appeal to the great detective himself. These may be dubbed 'The Case of the Missing Plaque' and 'The Adventure of the Baker Street Pillar Box'.

But to set the scene for early deliberations it is proper to recall that prior to the claims of Baker Street or the Midlands the creator of Sherlock Holmes had a debt to the city of Edinburgh. Here he was born, in May 1859, as the eldest son of a professional architect with some talent for painting, who was employed as deputy at the Office of Works in the city. The young Arthur Conan Doyle, after being educated at Hodder House preparatory school and the Jesuit-run public school of Stonyhurst College in Lancashire, returned to the city of his birth as a student at the University Medical School. It was while still a medical student at Edinburgh that the future author had his first professional engagement in the Midlands, in July of 1878.

By compressing a year's work into half a year it was permitted as part of the training for a medical degree for a student in need of an additional source of income to be employed by a practising doctor as a medical dispensary assistant. Conan Doyle was keen to pay his way and lend some financial assistance to his mother; his father's physical and mental condition, soon destined to deteriorate to the point of institutionalisation, was already giving cause for some concern.

Conan Doyle's first post as medical apprentice and dispenser, with a Dr Richardson in a poor quarter of Sheffield, had lasted just three weeks. This appointment, as its brevity suggests, had not proved a great success. Conan Doyle was reported to have summed up the experience by observing: 'these Sheffielders would rather be poisoned by a man with a beard than be saved by a man without one'. Conan Doyle's first appointment in the Midlands counties, which brought him to a small practice in rural Shropshire, was a little longer and somewhat more satisfying than the time with Dr Richardson in Yorkshire.

1

Conan Doyle and Shropshire

In the middle of 1878 Conan Doyle took up a post in Shropshire. As he tells us in *Memories and Adventures*, that year he had put out an advertisement in the medical press which ran along the lines of:- 'Third year's student, desiring experience rather than remuneration, offers his services'.[1] A response eventually came, as Conan Doyle was to record forty five years later:- 'It was from a Dr Elliot living in a townlet in Shropshire which rejoiced in the extraordinary name of "Ruyton-of-the-eleven-towns". It was not big enough to make one town, far less eleven'.[2]

Ruyton-XI-Towns is situated ten miles north-east of Shrewsbury, not far from the Welsh border, on the road to Oswestry and Holyhead. The nearest station on the old Great Western line to Manchester was Baschurch, two and a half miles to the east. The town retains an attractive, quiet rural character to this day, with buildings of the local red sandstone much in evidence in the long street of the village. It is indeed no more than a village, though once in medieval times, considered a manor, bringing together within its span eleven hamlets.

Conan Doyle had four months here with Dr Elliot of Cliffe House (the 'Cliffe' is pronounced to rhyme with 'knife', referring to the name of an adjacent hill). The easy-going practice in Ruyton seemed to have given Arthur the amount of freedom from duties he was never able to be availed of in the urban ones he worked at in Sheffield and later in Aston.

We know from the researches of Yoland Brown that Ruyton at that time would have had its social distractions for Conan Doyle. One source of modest appeal was a successful cricket club in the village, with a cricket pitch complete with a pavilion known locally, if

Cliffe House, as it is today.

uninvitingly, as The Cow House.[3] The man who would go on to play for the M.C.C. at Lords and bowl out the legendary W. G. Grace may well have had opportunity to be involved in this less illustrious context in the latter part of the 1878 season. And there were local dramatic productions in the village which invited talent and may have attracted the young Conan Doyle.

Conan Doyle might have found life quiet in Ruyton but it would not have been bereft of stimulation. The relaxed pace of life in the small community gave him time to think rather more freely than hitherto; the harsh regime of Stonyhurst College was a bitter recent memory and his rejection of Catholicism at least one source for serious reflection.

Another subject we know he concerned himself with while in Ruyton was that of alcoholism. Prompted perhaps by his father's own drinking problem which had led to the loss of his job and contributed to his eventual institutionalisation, young Conan Doyle penned an unsuccessful essay for a medico-literary competition on the effects of alcoholism which has never been published.[4] It seems to have been encouraged by Dr Elliot who, parish papers tell us, had some

Doctor's old surgery side entrance to Cliffe House, as it is today.

involvement with the local Temperance Society.[5] Evidence of the local press gives an indication that Conan Doyle would have had some primary source material for his essay, as Ruyton had its share of problems with the drunk and disorderly.[6]

Another diversion for Conan Doyle would have been walks in the nearby Welsh hills which, we are free to conjecture, might have provided the inspiration for the story 'That Veteran' published four years later. This contains some none too complimentary sentiments on the rural Welsh character.[7]

Later Conan Doyle looked back upon his short period in Shropshire as formative in his development:-

> It was a very quiet existence and I had a good deal of time to myself under very pleasant circumstances, so that I really trace some little mental progress to that period, for I read and thought without interruption. My medical duties were of a routine nature save on a few occasions.[8]

Ruyton may be adjudged important too in Conan Doyle's brief

medical career in that it was here that the first recorded reference is made to his treating a patient of his own, under dramatic sounding circumstances. As Conan Doyle relates it in *Memories and Adventures*:-

> The doctor was out when there came a half-crazed messenger to say that in some rejoicings in a neighbouring great house they had exploded an old cannon which had promptly burst and grievously injured one of the by-standers. No doctor was available, so I was the last resource. On arriving there I found a man in bed with a lump of iron sticking out of the side of his head. I tried not to show the alarm which I felt, and I did the obvious thing by pulling out the iron. I could see the clean white bone, so I could assure them that the brain had not been injured. I then pulled the gash together, staunched the bleeding, and finally bound it up, so that when the doctor did at last arrive he had little to add. This incident gave me confidence and, what is more important still, gave others confidence.[9]

It has been suggested by Yoland Brown that the 'neighbouring great house' was probably Park House, the location now of Packwood Haugh Preparatory School, a building standing on a hill just to the north of Ruyton, which had come under the ownership of Rev Thomas Henry Hunt. His family were, it seems, in the habit of letting off a piece of artillery at festive events, no doubt to the consternation of Dr Elliot's household.[10]

Henry Francis Elliot of Cliffe House, Ruyton had been resident physician at the Edinburgh Royal Infirmary and House Surgeon at Chichester Infirmary. From what can be gleaned from the few references to him in contemporary parish papers, while in Ruyton he took some active and eminently respectable part in local affairs. He served on a committee for the erection of a boundary wall for the extension of the churchyard,[11] and at the Oddfellows Fete in the summer of 1882 was numbered among other speakers who 'all did their best to do honour to the occasion by inculcating principles of loyalty, thrift, foresight, good fellowship, and order'.[12]

Dr Elliot was still to have a long medical career before him after Conan Doyle left his service. He seems to have moved from Ruyton in 1883 to a practice at Brook House, Wanstead East, where he was also to be surgeon of the Infant Orphanage Asylum.[13] He was

Packwood Haugh Preparatory School formerly Park House, site of Conan Doyle's first medical case.

subsequently in practice in Walthamstow and Chiswick, and died in Hove, Sussex in 1915 at the age of 69.[14]

In his memoirs published in the 1920s Conan Doyle was to say that he was happy at Ruyton and had pleasing recollections of Dr Elliot and his wife.[15] But this may have been an example of distance lending a degree of enchantment. If we accept the accounts of biographers who had access to certain family papers since cut off to researchers the sojourn in Ruyton had its quota of friction. Conan Doyle is reported to have referred to the doctor as bad tempered and likely to explode in response to the tritest of passing remarks.[16] Dr Elliot, Conan Doyle apparently observed, had not an original idea in his head, being quite liable to fly into a rage if anyone happened to be bold enough to advance one. When Arthur put forward the proposition that capital punishment should be abolished Dr Elliot 'went into a fury', forbidding any such subversive remarks from being uttered in the house again. Conan Doyle was said to have spiritedly retorted that he would air his opinions 'when and where I liked'.[17] One imagines that the relationship between the two men was considerably strained thereafter.

7

When Conan Doyle asked for his train fare to return to Edinburgh from Dr Elliot the doctor was alleged to have replied 'My dear fellow, the law stands thus. If an assistant has a salary, he is then a recognised person and can claim expenses. But if he has no salary he becomes as it were, a gentleman travelling for his own improvement; he gets nothing'.[18] It is not too much to surmise that there is more than a touch of Dr Elliot in the character of the miserly Dr Oldacre in Conan Doyle's story 'The Croxley Master', published in *The Strand* in 1899.[19] A medical assistant, Robert Montgomery, struggling to qualify for his degree while working for a practising doctor somewhere in the north of England, asks his employer, a Dr Oldacre, to advance him money for his class fees, even offering to pay appropriate interest on it. The response is an indignant refusal unmistakably reminiscent of Dr Elliot's own snub to Conan Doyle, and Montgomery is forced to turn to prize-fighting (one of Conan Doyle's own passions) for the necessary additional income. But to do justice to Dr Elliot, we might recall that Conan Doyle's advertisement for employment had done something to invite a niggardly response from a prospective employer, since the aspiring young medical student was, to repeat his own words, 'desiring experience rather than remuneration'.

An even less flattering possibility than the suggestion that Dr Elliot was the model for Dr Oldacre is that he became the model for Dr Grimesby Roylott in one of the early Sherlock Holmes stories (and, incidentally, the one Conan Doyle was to rate as the best). In 'The Adventure of the Speckled Band', set in 1883, the surname of the formidable and quick-tempered villain (abbreviated to Rylott in the successful stage play of the story Conan Doyle wrote some years later) does suggest a compound of the name of Ruyton and Elliot.[20] We might charitably regard this as fanciful. Though it may be seen that *The Strand* illustrations of Dr Oldacre and Dr Roylott produced by Sidney Paget bear some striking similarities, there is no record of the upstanding Dr Elliot of Ruyton keeping a baboon, cheetah or deadly swamp adder as did the odious Dr Roylott.

It may have been while still in Shropshire that Conan Doyle first became aware of a real life crime which had taken place in that particular county fifty years before. It is a case which in the annals of treachery arguably exceeded anything Holmes was to encounter and may have helped Conan Doyle form the opinion he was to put into the mouth of Sherlock Holmes in 'The Copper Beeches': 'It is my belief,

"I AM GRIEVED AND DISAPPOINTED, MR. MONTGOMERY."

"WHICH OF YOU IS HOLMES?"

Dr Oldacre confronts the medical student Montgomery in 'The Croxley Master'.	Dr Grimesby Roylott confronts Sherlock Holmes in 'The Adventure of the Speckled Band'.

Illustrations from *The Strand*

Watson, founded upon my experience, that the lowest and vilest alleys in London do not present a more dreadful record of sin than does the smiling and beautiful countryside'.[21] Just over ten years after leaving Shropshire and two years after the first appearance of Sherlock Holmes Conan Doyle was to publish a detailed account of 'The Bravoes of Market Drayton' in *Chambers's Journal*.[22] 'Neither in the dens of Whitechapel nor in the slums of Birmingham was morality so lax or human life so cheap' says Conan Doyle here of the quiet rural Shropshire of cider orchards and sheep-walks where a large section of the peasant population, often linked by blood and marriage, could successfully band together to defy the law.

The case in point involved a Shropshire peasant, Thomas Ellson, who had been arrested in Market Drayton for stealing sheep, a hanging offence in 1827. The prosecution broke down when the chief witness disappeared, murdered by 'bravoes' put up to it by Ellson's mother and father-in-law.

After his release Ellson was caught fowl-stealing, and in order to escape the trifling punishment due him denounced his relatives and friends for the murder of the chief witness at the sheep-theft trial. 'No more repulsive spectacle has ever been witnessed in an English court of justice', wrote Conan Doyle of Ellson quite imperturbably giving the evidence which would get his mother and father-in-law transported and his brother-in-law and another associate hanged for having gone to such a terrible extremity to save his life. Ellson was made to witness the executions as a warning to him to mend his ways. As Conan Doyle put it, seemingly now better disposed towards capital punishment:-

> The air of the Shropshire downs was the sweeter for the dispersal of the precious band; and it is on record that this salutary example brought it home to the rustics that the law was still a power in the land, and that, looking upon it as a mere commercial transaction, the trade of the bravo was not one which could flourish upon English soil.

[1] A. Conan Doyle, *Memories and Adventures*, (Hodder and Stoughton, 1924), p. 28.
[2] ibid., p. 28.
[3] Yoland Brown, *Ruyton XI Towns: Unusual Name, Unusual History*, (Brewin, 1988), p. 125.
[4] Pierre Nordon, *Conan Doyle*, (John Murray, 1966), trans. Francis Partridge, pp. 25-26.
[5] ibid., and see *Parish Notes For Ellesmere 1879-1883*, 'The Ellesmere Ruridecanal Magazine', The Vicar of Penley (ed.), April 1881, p. 67.
[6] Prosecutions for drunkenness in Ruyton reported in *The Shrewsbury Chronicle*, 9.7.1878, 23.8.1878, 14.10.1878 and 22.11.1878. But also see Brown, op. cit., pp. 124-125 suggesting local sobriety.
[7] A. Conan Doyle, 'That Veteran', *All The Year Round*, 2.9.1882 and reprinted in J.M. Gibson and R.L. Green (eds.), *The Unknown Conan Doyle: Uncollected Stories*, (Secker and Warburg, 1982), pp. 64-74.
[8] Conan Doyle, *Memories*, op. cit., p. 28.
[9] ibid., p. 28.
[10] Brown, op. cit., p. 93.
[11] *Parish Notes*, op. cit., April 1879, p. 42.
[12] ibid., August 1882, p. 127.
[13] *Medical Directory*, 1878-1915.
[14] ibid., and see A. E. Rodin and C. Roden, 'Arthur Conan Doyle, Dr Elliot and Ruyton-XI-Towns', *Journal of the Arthur Conan Doyle Society*, Vol. 2,

Number 1, Spring 1991, pp. 15–26.

[15]Conan Doyle, *Memories*, op. cit., p. 28.

[16]J. Dickson Carr, *The Life of Sir Arthur Conan Doyle*, (John Murray, 1949), pp. 37–38.

[17]Dickson Carr, op. cit., pp. 37–38 and Nordon, op. cit. quotes Conan Doyle's letter to his mother on the incident, p. 184.

[18]Dickson Carr, op. cit., p. 38.

[19]A. Conan Doyle, 'The Croxley Master', *Strand*, October-December 1899.

[20]A. Conan Doyle, 'The Adventure of the Speckled Band', *Strand*, February 1892 and *The Adventures of Sherlock Holmes*, (Newnes, 1892).

[21]A. Conan Doyle, 'The Adventure of the Copper Beeches'. *Strand*, June 1892 and *The Adventures of Sherlock Holmes*, (Newnes, 1892).

[22]A. Conan Doyle, 'The Bravoes of Market Drayton', *Chambers's Journal*, 24.8.1889. It is also worth adding here that Charlotte Stoneham, who was to marry the Rev Shapurji Edalji and become the mother of George Edalji—whose case Conan Doyle was to take up in 1906 (a matter discussed in chapter 3)—came from Ketley in Shropshire, where her father was vicar.

2

Conan Doyle and Aston

After Ruyton-XI-Towns Conan Doyle's next medical engagement was also to be in the Midlands, with a Dr Reginald Ratcliff Hoare in Aston, a manor on the north-east corner of Birmingham. Aston was to be absorbed as a suburb of the rapidly growing city of Birmingham in 1911, and is now thought of as very much an inner urban area. The move to Dr Hoare's practice in Clifton House, Aston Road North was to have important consequences for Conan Doyle: his time in the area of Birmingham, like that of Dr Johnson's back in the 1730s, saw his first published work and signalled the beginnings of an illustrious literary career.

Conan Doyle was to work for Dr Hoare for several spells, the first from the middle of 1879 till February 1880, and he was to work for him a final time briefly in early 1882, making short return visits of a social nature to the Hoare family thereafter. He was away from Aston for lengthy periods between 1879 and 1882 including two highly eventful voyages — seven months on board a Greenland whaler as a doctor from March to October 1880 and a period as a medical man on a ship around the coast of West Africa ending in January 1882.

Like Dr Elliot of Ruyton, Dr Hoare of Aston had medical connections with Edinburgh, becoming a Fellow of the Royal College of Surgeons, Edinburgh in 1879, the same year young Conan Doyle was to join him.[1] Dr Hoare was then in his mid-thirties and a highly successful medical practitioner whose ménage included a cook, a housemaid, a coachman and a groom, as well as a turnover of medical assistants.[2] Among his appointments were those of Honorary Surgeon to the Industrial School, Gem Street, and Honorary Medical Officer to the Aston Fire Brigade.[3] Conan Doyle in his *Memories and Adventures* writes of Dr Hoare as a well-known Birmingham doctor

> who had a five horse city practice, and as every working doctor, before the days of motors, would realise...this meant going from morning to night. He earned some £3,000 a year, which takes some doing, when it is collected from 3s 6d visits and 1s 6d bottles of medicine, among the very poorest classes of Aston. Hoare was a fine fellow, stout, square, red-faced, bushy-whiskered and dark-eyed. His wife was also a very kindly and gifted woman, and my position in the house was soon rather that of a son than of an assistant.[4]

There was a shared partiality for tobacco. Mrs Hoare enjoyed a cigar, and Conan Doyle and Dr Hoare were fond of a pipe. Probably Conan Doyle had Dr Hoare in mind when he wrote in his autobiographical novel *The Stark Munro Letters*, in which the figure of Dr Horton is a thinly disguised Dr Hoare, of the 'most abandoned smoker I have ever met with, collecting the dottles of his pipes in the evening, and smoking them the next morning before breakfast in the stable yard'.[5] We might recall here how Dr Watson finds Sherlock Holmes in 'The Adventure of the Engineer's Thumb', just as he expects to, 'smoking his before breakfast pipe, which was composed of all the plugs and dottles left from his smokes the day before, all carefully dried and collected on the corner of the mantlepiece'.[6]

The adopted status Conan Doyle enjoyed in the Hoare household didn't mean the young medical student, still only 20 years old, was given an easy time of things — far from it. The work of dispensing prescriptions, sometimes as many as a hundred bottles in an evening, he described as 'hard and incessant'. The pay was, as Conan Doyle ironically remarked, 'a real money making proposition to the extent of some two pounds a month'.[7]

Not only did Dr Hoare take warmly to Conan Doyle as a person, he evidently had a high regard for his medical competence: as well as the dispensing of medicines, entrusting him with an increasing number of midwifery cases, and some more serious cases in the general practice. Something of the day's routine at the Hoares' might be guessed at from *The Stark Munro Letters* and it was clearly somewhat gruelling. Work at the surgery was at full swing at 9.30 a.m. with breaks at lunch, then the rounds began which involved venturing into the great shabby rows of monotonous terraces, and back for tea when the evening work of

Dr Reginald Ratcliff Hoare, Conan Doyle's employer in Aston.

dispensing medicines and fresh advice might not allow time for recreation till 10.00 p.m.[8] Conan Doyle had his own list of the poorer patients of the practice to visit and in the area of Aston 'saw a great deal, for better or worse, of very low life'.[9] It is reasonable to observe that his experiences down the mean streets of Aston helped him write so convincingly in the Sherlock Holmes tales about the Victorian lower classes.

Conan Doyle's father had lost his job, a reverse attributable to excessive drinking, a couple of years before Arthur came to work for Dr Hoare, and thereafter appears to have declined into alcoholism and

15

Conan Doyle about the time of his employment in Aston.

epilepsy. Soon after Conan Doyle came to Birmingham for his final period with Dr Hoare his father was institutionalised — first in a home for alcoholics, subsequently one for epileptics — dying ten years later.[10]

Some additional responsibility lay upon what young Conan Doyle could earn. With his father an invalid, he found himself head of a large family; though it was 'genteel poverty' which threatened, rather than the 'low life' he witnessed at such close quarters in the backstreets of Aston.

Conan Doyle's generosity of nature seems not to have been undermined by such economic pressures judging from an incident recorded by both Dickson Carr and Nordon.[11] One afternoon, as he made up sixty or so bottles of medicine in Dr Hoare's dispensary, an Arabian and Sanskrit scholar by name of Gleiwitz approached him in tears, to explain that his own family were reduced to a good deal more than genteel poverty: they were starving. Gleiwitz had lost what capital he had had through some bad investments and had come to rely on giving German lessons to support his household, and now had only one pupil, Mrs Amy Hoare. Conan Doyle apparently had just 1s 6d in his pocket but gave the German his watch and chain, assuring the scholar that he was free to pawn it.

During his time in Aston Conan Doyle first realised money was to be earned from writing. He records in *Memories and Adventures* his early forays into the realms of literature:-

Some friend remarked to me that my letters were very vivid and surely I could write some things to sell. I may say that the general inspiration towards literature was tremendously strong upon me, and that my mind was reaching out in what seemed an aimless way in all sorts of directions. I used to be allowed 2d for my lunch, that being the price of a mutton pie, but near the pie shop was a second-hand bookshop with a barrel full of old books and the legend 'Your Choice for 2d' stuck above it. Often the price of my luncheon used to be spent on some sample out of this barrel, and I have within reach of my arm as I write these lines, copies of Gordon's *Tacitus*, Temple's *Works*, Pope's *Homer*, Addison's *Spectator* and Swift's *Works*, which all came out of the twopenny box. Anyone observing my actions and tastes would have said that so strong a spring would certainly overflow, but for my own part I never dreamed I could myself produce decent prose, and the remark of my friend, who was by no means given to flattery, took me greatly by surprise. I sat down, however, and wrote a little adventure story which I called 'The Mystery of the Sassasa Valley'. To my great joy and surprise it was accepted by *Chambers' Journal*, and I received three guineas. It mattered not that other attempts failed. I had done it once and I cheered myself by the thought that I could do it again. It was years before I touched *Chambers'* again, but in 1879 I had a story, 'The American's Tale', in *London Society* for which also I got a small cheque. But the idea of real success was far from my mind.[12]

(It is just about worth remarking that Pope's *Homer* crops up in the Holmes story 'The Reigate Squires'. A copy is stolen in what appears a casual robbery but it transpires is motivated by a rival squire's search for

17

documents relating to a lawsuit — I will not labour the fact that the murder in the story is of a coachman called William, the name of the groom in the Hoares' household).[13] The products of the reject box didn't say much for the Birmingham folk's feel for good literature — or maybe a more kindly interpretation is that it indicated something of an uncommon surfeit of it.

A prime candidate for the friend who suggested to young Conan Doyle a writing career is the nephew of Dr Hoare and a fellow assistant in the Clifton House practice, Rupert Hoare Hunter, a man who was to operate a medical practice in Sutton Street, not far from Clifton House, for over twenty years.[14] Hunter was full of encouragement as the result of seeing Arthur's letters and stories written for Dr Hoare's children.[15]

Long though the hours of work for Dr Hoare were, there was encouragement to write and an abundance of energy on Conan Doyle's part to make use of what free time he did get to serve his apprenticeship to fiction writing. In his first stint with Dr Hoare Conan Doyle published that early story 'The Mystery of the Sassasa Valley', set in South Africa and featuring the finding of a hidden diamond.[16] By the time he finally left Birmingham Conan Doyle had several more published works to his credit.

Conan Doyle published the first of his many letters to the press while in Aston, a letter which revealed him engaged in administering to himself drug overdoses in the cause of medical research.[17] In the *British Medical Journal* of September 1879 he related his experiments with a drug called gelsemium, the dried root of yellow jasmine, an alkaloid stimulant with apparently similar effects to nicotine but, as Rodin and Key say, 'With a stronger central depressant action'.[18] Though no longer prescribed in Britain today by orthodox medical practitioners, in the 1870s gelsemium was made much use of by doctors, being recommended for pleurisy, pneumonia, yellow fever and neuralgia — it was taken by Conan Doyle initially for the persistent effects of the latter. He recorded how he increasingly overstepped the maximum recommended textbook dosage in the course of a week to the point even his robust constitution was put at risk. Before Conan Doyle's experiments a number of deaths from respiratory arrest had been reported from doses far smaller than he subjected himself to.[19]

His determination to test to the limit a dangerous drug perhaps suggests a greater commitment to the pursuit of medical knowledge than he was usually prepared to acknowledge he had. Probably Rodin and

Key are to an extent correct to think there was much of the dramatic gesture about Conan Doyle's experiments with gelsemium.[20] There was much in it too of a characteristic he was to lend to his famous sleuth. In *The Sign of Four* we first learn of Holmes's own drug habit and its necessary antidote in the work of problem-solving. Holmes tells Watson, 'My mind rebels at stagnation.... I abhor the dull routine of existence. I crave for mental stimulation. That is why I have chosen my own particular profession, or rather created it...'.[21]

Certainly Rodin and Key are right to evaluate Conan Doyle an unlikely suicide.[22] And he was, to give him his due, evidently in full control of what he was doing in turning what had begun as his own neuralgic affliction to the benefit of published medical research. If it was a dramatic gesture it was not a vainglorious one. Conan Doyle was also in a good position to understand what was involved in the habit he gave to Sherlock Holmes when he resorts to his famous seven per cent solution of cocaine 'as a protest against the monotony of existence when cases were scanty and the papers uninteresting'.[23]

From what can be gathered Conan Doyle seems to have had at least one serious relationship with a local Aston girl. This was, however, actively discouraged by his mother and by Dr and Amy Hoare, and their considerable influence prevailed.[24]

With the hectic nature of the work Conan Doyle had to do for Dr Hoare it was surprising he found a sufficiency of time for writing or anything else. But once free of the burden of being a medical student — his final oral exams were in June 1881 — Conan Doyle came to devote more time to creative work.

In 1882 Conan Doyle returned to a branch of Dr Hoare's practice after his adventures as a ship's doctor off the coast of Africa. These few months, February to April 1882, he stayed at 'The Elms', Gravelly Hill, about two miles up the road from the Aston Road North surgery, near to Six Ways, Erdington and just to the north of where the Gravelly Hill Interchange, more evocatively known as Spaghetti Junction, lies today.[25] 'The Elms' had become for a time another part of Dr Hoare's practice.[26] Here Sam Aspinall, a 30 year old medical surgeon and brother-in-law to Dr Hoare was resident and partner in practice to the elder, more experienced doctor still based at Clifton House.[27] Aspinall was for many years to run a surgery in his own right at 'The Greylands, just across the road from 'The Elms'.[28]

Conan Doyle's renewed efforts in writing after his return to the

Conan Doyle and Aston

Front view of 'The Elms',
Gravelly Hill, as it is today,
and rear view,
with old stables on right.

Midlands, included an account of his African experiences for the *British Journal of Photography*, and stories such as 'Bones', 'The Actor's Duel' and 'My Friend The Murderer'. He also found time to write a learned letter to the Lancet, 'Notes on a Case of Leucocythaemia' which in his diagnosis and analysis of a disease now better known as leukaemia some might detect a soupçon of the method of Conan Doyle's future immortal creation.[29]

Life at the Hoares appears not to have been entirely consumed by serious preoccupations if we are to judge from the testimony of the son of Rupert Hoare Hunter, Rupert Doyle Hunter. One practical joke of Conan Doyle's was said by Mr Hunter to have resulted in a stern warning from the local constabulary of Aston. Conan Doyle had allegedly sent out hundreds of gilt-edged invitation cards to a non-existent Mayor's ball.[30] It has been objected that at that time he was unlikely to have been able to afford such an extravagant jape. But, such an objection notwithstanding, it is true to say that the streak of mischievous humour is a rather critically neglected aspect of Conan Doyle's writing; and, as we shall presently see, there is some reason for suspecting references in the Holmes stories have a number of in-jokes relating to his Midland experiences.

Those who venture to Aston Road North today will, thanks to massive redevelopment involving flyovers, expressways and interchanges, find little of the Aston Conan Doyle had known. Clifton House itself has been gutted and virtually rebuilt. Conan Doyle would have been familiar with the old clock tower of Aston Cross, the design of which was based on the Jacobean architecture of nearby Aston Hall, but the less imposing one that stands there to this day was erected in 1891.

Less than three-quarters of a mile up the road, uneasily beside the Aston Expressway, there are the surviving splendours of Aston Hall. And there yet stands Aston Parish Church on Witton Lane. This church has an interesting association with the detective genre in that ten years after Conan Doyle left Aston a young Ronald Knox, who was to become no mean writer of detective stories himself, came to live there, his father having taken over as vicar, having previously been rector of St Philip's Church in Birmingham city centre. Knox was to write a catalogue of rules for detective story writing and become something of a Sherlock Holmes connoisseur, publishing a donnish tongue-in-cheek essay entitled 'Studies in the Literature of Sherlock Holmes'.[31]

More recently, in the early 1950s, when there was still a great deal of

Aston Cross as Conan Doyle would have known it.

the squalor of old Aston remaining that Conan Doyle must have known so well in the late 1870s, an insurance agent named Ronald Pearsall was based near the Aston Cross clock tower just a few yards from Clifton House and in his duties he covered much of the territory that would have been covered by Conan Doyle when a medical assistant. Pearsall went on to become a biographer of Conan Doyle and even to publish his own contribution to Sherlock Holmes fiction.[32]

In early 1882 Conan Doyle became partner to Dr Budd, a man he describes briefly in *Memories and Adventures*, and who appears in *The Stark Munro Letters* under the name of Cullingworth. Budd was to have a somewhat sinister role in Conan Doyle's life. They had taken their exams and qualified in Edinburgh at the same time. Early in 1882 Budd invited Conan Doyle to join him in practice in Plymouth with the promise of a guaranteed income of £300 a year. The result was a short-lived association with nothing like the promised income accruing to Conan Doyle. The two fell out, precipitated apparently by a letter from Conan Doyle's mother denouncing Budd, which the latter had surreptitiously read.

Budd's father had been an outstanding medical man, pioneering such important aspects of public health as sewerage sanitation in the prevention of cholera epidemics and the necessity for a fresh clean water supply. But Budd had no such claims to eminence, indeed there seems to have been a strong element of the charlatan about him, embodied in published pieces for the *British Medical Journal*.[33]

Dudley Edwards in *The Quest for Sherlock Holmes*[34] suggests Budd, in subsequently inducing Conan Doyle to a practice further along the coast at Southsea, was concocting a Moriarty-like ploy to bring the young medical man to bankruptcy and ruination. For this practice was one Budd knew was failing. The plot, if it were such, backfired because Conan Doyle could employ himself in the hours of leisure resulting from an empty surgery with the work which was to gain him literary fame.

As Dudley Edwards suggests, one impulse behind Conan Doyle's going to Southsea, indeed in having any further truck with Budd after the way the man had treated him, was to rebel against possessiveness. Here he might strike out for an independence he lacked in a succession of relationships with 'father-figures', including Joseph Bell of Edinburgh, oft regarded as the prototype for Sherlock Holmes, Dr Hoare of Aston, and Budd himself; eventually it was to be that 'the boy they tried to make their Watson wove them remorselessly and inescapably into his Holmes'. Conan Doyle ignored the well-meaning advice from Dr Hoare and in so doing was spurred to a new self-reliance.[35]

He was not to return to live at Dr Hoare's house after the move to Southsea. He was to miss the smallpox epidemic of 1883 in Aston which resulted in a public outcry against inadequate facilities and led to the establishment of the Hospital for Infectious Diseases, Witton.

Clifton House was used as late as 1955 as a doctor's surgery. In the late 1950s it was taken over by an old neighbour from the late nineteenth century, which had then been a firm of coach builders, Thomas Startin's Motors. It was vacated by Startin's in 1989 and is at the time of writing advertised to let.

Dr Hoare did acquire a house just around the corner at 24 Sutton Street in 1894 (now demolished) but continued to keep on his surgery at Clifton House till his death in 1898 whereupon it was taken over briefly by his son, Dr Reginald Cecil Hoare.[36]

Dr Hoare's only published work, which appeared in 1880, was prompted, as Dudley Edwards shows, by what he saw as Budd's detrimental influence.[37] When Dr Hoare, seeing himself in loco parentis to Conan Doyle, found a poorly researched article by Budd in the *British Medical Journal* the perfect opportunity to effect some retribution presented itself.

If we are reluctant to deny the testimony of Conan Doyle himself that Joseph Bell in Edinburgh was the model for Holmes it would also be hard to deny that Hoare also played some small part in the inspiration, as the letter Hoare published on the hallowed subject of gout in the *British Medical Journal* surely gives an indication:-

> Few will be found willing to dispute Mr Budd's proposition, that there is a law of compensation between the various organs of the body; when, however, he propounds a new pathological doctrine founded upon this basis, he is perhaps a little too sanguine. Our physiological knowledge of the lymphatic system, and of its functions in our economy, is not exact enough to warrant our laying down hard and fast pathological rules in regard to it. Mr Budd's application of Chrzonszczewsky's experiment, where, after tying the ureters, he discovered urates in the connective tissue corpuscles, is extremely ingenious. He is, however, hardly justified in drawing a deduction of his own, and ignoring the interpretation put upon the fact by the eminent Russian physiologist. Chrzonszczewsky, if I remember right, considered that the experiment proved the origin of urates from the connective tissue corpuscles; while Mr Budd quotes it as conclusive evidence that matter is drained away into the lymph-channels when the kidney is unable to excrete it. The corpuscles, too, can hardly be called lymphatic, as the views of Recklinghausen are now pretty well generally accepted, which maintain that the spaces in fibrous tissue are the true starting-points of the lymphatic vessels.
>
> Apart from the physiological facts, we cannot see how Mr Budd can answer certain objections to his novel theory. How is it, we would ask, that other noxious material circulating in the blood, and requiring elimination, does not produce the same train of symptoms? What is the subtle connection between uric acid, in particular, and the lymphatics? If the disease be due to the breaking down of an eliminative system, and subsequent congestion of the part, why should one agent alone be able to produce it? In spite of objections, there can, however, be no doubt that Mr Budd has advanced a bold and original theory, and one capable of far wider application. Pathologists will welcome any rational explanation founded upon a

true scientific basis, and not dependent upon pure hypothesis, or upon deductions from organic chemistry.[38]

This devastating critique of Budd in the *British Medical Journal* of 25 December 1880 was the turning point in Budd's pretensions. Crushing victory as it was for Dr Hoare, paradoxically it may well have stimulated a feeling of sympathy for Budd in Conan Doyle, contributing to eventually directing his steps to the south coast.

The time Conan Doyle spent with Dr Hoare was vital to his development. As we have seen, here he was to find valuable inspiration and witness the first publication of his writing. In some of Conan Doyle's early stories of the 1880s Birmingham can be recognised in 'Birchespool', the name probably constructed, as Dudley Edwards claims, from *Bir*mingham, Man*ches*ter, and Liver*pool*.[39] The author did seem to have had a liking for names made up of artful compounds, what Lewis Carroll called 'portmanteau' words. In Conan Doyle's *The Stark Munro Letters* 'Birchespool' is based on Southsea but the character of Dr Horton in this work can be identified with Dr Hoare. (It is open to speculation whether the name of Horton was derived from the chemist George Day Horton then operating across the road from Clifton House at 68 Aston Road North — evidence from the Holmes stories suggests Conan Doyle had fondness for jokes of this kind.)

Monseignor Ronald Knox, not averse to acknowledging his own association with Birmingham, in a radio talk published as 'Birmingham Revisited', testifies that the city 'true to its manufacturing instincts...takes over the unfinished article, moulds it, refines it, and re-exports it dignified, for-ever, with her trade-mark'.[40] Knox cites individuals who were not raw products of the city but were transformed by the experience of living there — James Watt, Joseph Priestley, John Bright, Joe Chamberlain. As a Sherlockian who had lived in Aston Knox might have been expected to mention Conan Doyle as bearing something of the city's trademark, but does not. Conan Doyle's experience in the area of Birmingham, as Dudley Edwards, with justification says, 'was clearly seminal, more so than it is probably possible for us to chart'.[41]

When Conan Doyle left Dr Hoare's practice for the south coast in 1882 he and the Hoare family remained in touch by letter. This correspondence furnishes ample evidence of just how strong a bond of friendship had been created during Conan Doyle's time in Aston.[42] The author was even to believe it had survived the grave. For as late as 1921 we find Conan Doyle writing to Dr Hoare's daughter Josephine, a sympathiser with his spiritualist opinions, telling her of just how conscious he was of the presence of Dr Hoare's wife, Amy, who had recently died.[43]

Conan Doyle was to revisit the Hoare family in Aston to some literary consequence, and Dr Hoare was to visit Conan Doyle on the south coast.[44] And during Dr Hoare's final illness he and Amy paid a visit of some weeks duration to the home of Conan Doyle in the hope that the change might benefit the ailing medical man.[45] It was not to be. At Dr Hoare's funeral in March 1898 among floral tributes from Aston Fire Brigade and the tramways employees a beautiful wreath was received from Conan Doyle.[46]

Dr Hoare's funeral at Witton Cemetery was reportedly attended by many of the medical men of the neighbourhood, and almost certainly present was Dr David Holmes. Perhaps a startling debt of Conan Doyle's to Birmingham would be that the surname of his legendary detective was suggested by that rival doctor to Dr Hoare who was practising just a few yards up the road from Clifton House at 33 Lichfield Road, later 39 Lichfield Road, (now demolished), from the mid-1880s.[47] Conan Doyle may very well have heard of Dr Holmes from the Hoare family at the time of conceiving *A Study In Scarlet*, the novel which first introduced Sherlock Holmes to the world, published in 1887. Dr Holmes was to work in Aston for some twenty years and held the post of deputy coroner for the county of Warwickshire.[48] As David Holmes graduated from the University of Edinburgh in 1877 it is just possible he was known to Conan Doyle even then.

To complete the connection of the name of the great detective with the Birmingham area the interesting suggestion can be added (but not corroborated) that Conan Doyle was aware of a seller of violins in the fatefully named Sherlock Street, Birmingham.[49] This particular street, which runs for over half a mile into the south central part of the city not far from the Bull Ring, had its origins with Thomas Sherlock, Bishop of London. In the early eighteenth century Sherlock bought land in Edgbaston for speculative purposes. This was inherited by his nephew, who was responsible for naming Thomas and Bishop as well as Sherlock Street in remembrance of his late uncle. It is a street which Conan Doyle would surely have known.

When Conan Doyle was writing *A Study In Scarlet* during the spring of 1886 he could not have guessed that he was creating one of the most

Grave of the Hoare family in Witton Cemetary, Birmingham.

famous fictional characters in the language. Not that the early indications were that immortality was assured. *A Study In Scarlet* was not rapturously received. Nor could it be said Sherlock Holmes had become a household name with the next published adventure of the detective, *The Sign of Four*, appearing three years later. It was the serialisation of the short stories in *The Strand* magazine beginning in July 1891, to be grouped collectively under the title of *The Adventures of Sherlock Holmes*,

27

Street sign in Sherlock Street, Birmingham today.

which first brought real fame for Conan Doyle's creation. In the Holmes stories which followed Birmingham was to be used as an actual setting for a story just once, though the city is alluded to several times.

The Hound of the Baskervilles, arguably the most famous of all the Sherlock Holmes tales, has strong Midland connections. Mention will later be made of the contribution of the Herefordshire Baskervilles and their neighbours the Vaughans to this novel.[50] A further posthumous spur to the use of the Baskerville name in the tale might well have been provided by the best remembered member of the Baskerville clan, the printer and inventor John Baskerville of Easy Row, Birmingham (1706 – 1775), who is celebrated today by the Civic Building, Baskerville House in Birmingham city centre, close to where his original house stood. For the various burials and disinterments of Baskerville were newsworthy matters, having become topical again at the time the author was contemplating *The Hound of the Baskervilles*, and would have been of particular interest to a connoisseur of the macabre like Conan Doyle. Though sufficiently well known, the adventures of Baskerville's corpse bear repeating.

When John Baskerville died the clergy denied him burial in a

Civic Building, Baskerville House, Birmingham in the summer of 1991, with
John Baskerville's monument in the foreground.

churchyard because of his atheistical views. His body was in 1821
removed from its first burial site, in the grounds of his house, and for
eight years lay in a warehouse where a charge was made to view the
remarkably well preserved cadaver. It was subsequently smuggled into
the vaults in Christ Church, on the corner of the present New Street and
Colmore Row.[51] In April 1893 much local newspaper coverage was
excited by the rediscovery and re-opening of Baskerville's coffin in
Christ Church catacombs.[52] Later that same year Conan Doyle revisited
the Hoare family in Aston during a lecture tour of the region and it is
quite possible he heard of the latest in the saga of Baskerville's body at
that time.[53]

In February 1898, with the redevelopment of Birmingham city centre
under way, Christ Church came under a demolition order, and the body
of Baskerville was then once more on the move. Baskerville's wife lay in
the churchyard of St Philip's where by this time the young Ronald
Knox's father was rector. But Mr and Mrs Baskerville were not to be
reunited. There is some controversy about the fate of John Baskerville's

John Baskerville of Birmingham (1706 – 1775).

remains thereafter. One version is that the body was claimed by a relative and taken off to the Black Country for reburial.[54] The more generally accepted view is that it was dispatched to Warstone Lane cemetery in Birmingham's Jewellery Quarter, where it rests to this day.[55]

John Baskerville's final posthumous adventures might have won the attention of the author of Sherlock Holmes then for an additional reason. Conan Doyle's thoughts were turned towards Birmingham because of the death, just a month after Baskerville's disinterment, of his old employer and long-time friend, Dr Reginald Ratcliff Hoare. It is more customary to regard the name of Baskerville as having been inspired by the name of his host's coachman when the author was on a visit to Devonshire. All in all the case for the Birmingham derivation of Baskerville seems at least as worthy of consideration.

As we shall see, Conan Doyle did make something fruitful out of a return visit to stay with the Hoares at Aston in December 1890. It was the month of the publication of the story 'The Surgeon of Gaster Fell', about a hard working doctor from Birmingham who has suffered a mental breakdown which leaves him prone to outbreaks of homicidal and religious mania.[56] Apparently this was not taken too personally and Conan Doyle's stop-off in the city on this occasion probably gave him the necessary material background for the Holmes story 'The Adventure of the Stockbroker's Clerk'.[57]

But near fatal were the consequences of the return to Birmingham to acquire a motor car in the spring of 1903. The automobile episode appears to have begun light-heartedly enough when Conan Doyle stepped from the train at New Street station splendidly attired for his new recreation in long-coat, yachting cap and goggles, only to be mistaken for a railway attendant by a lady enquiring the next train to Walsall.[58] Conan Doyle had come to purchase a dark blue twelve horse power Wolseley car with red wheels, to give him what he called 'a new interest in life'. His daredevil attitude to motoring combining with the drawbacks of the vehicle almost led to the author losing all interest in life.[59]

The following year, at a time when *Strand* readers were still enjoying the series of adventures featuring Sherlock Holmes revivified after his 'death' in the Reichenbach Falls, the Wolseley ran up a bank and overturned with the author pinned beneath it. The steering wheel bore some of the burden of the car but as it gave way the vehicle's weight was supposed to have actually settled on Conan Doyle shortly before a group could gather to lift the car off him.[60] He claimed that but for the lessons he had received from Sandow the famous strong man of the period he would not have cheated death. If it is true to say that Conan Doyle was to some degree 'Made in Birmingham' he was also very nearly unmade by it. Ten years later the experience of the car crash became enshrined in a story called 'How It Happened', in which the victim of just such an accident as Conan Doyle endured finds he has died and become a disembodied spirit.[61]

Before going on to discuss Sherlock Holmes's adventures in connection with the Midlands, which bring him to Herefordshire, Derbyshire and Birmingham, we will first take pause to deal with Conan Doyle's further involvement with the region after the great fictional sleuth had become an established part of national life. This involvement offers some examples of Conan Doyle taking an investigative role which invites comparison with the methods of his creation, Sherlock Holmes. In these real life cases friendships Conan Doyle struck up with Birmingham University men, Professor John Churton Collins and Sir Oliver Lodge, near neighbours of each other in Edgbaston, contributed some part. Churton Collins, Professor of English Literature at the University, best remembered today, if at all, for Tennyson's dismissal of him as 'a louse in the locks of literature', was a keen amateur criminologist and encouraged Conan Doyle's campaign on behalf of George Edalji, which is discussed in the next chapter.[62] And in the development of Conan Doyle's investigations into the mysteries of the spirit world it will be seen in chapter four that Sir Oliver Lodge, Principal of Birmingham University, was to be a major influence.

[1]*Medical Directory*, 1880.

[2]*Census*, 1881.

[3]*Medical Directory*, op. cit.

[4]A. Conan Doyle, *Memories and Adventures*, (Hodder and Stoughton, 1924), pp. 28 – 29.

[5]A. Conan Doyle, *The Stark Munro Letters*, (Longmans, Green and Co, 1895), pp. 94.

[6]A. Conan Doyle, 'The Adventure of the Engineer's Thumb', *Strand*, March 1892 and *The Adventures of Sherlock Holmes*, (Newnes, 1892).

[7]Conan Doyle, *Memories*, op. cit., p. 28.

[8]Conan Doyle, *Stark Munro Letters*, op. cit., p. 91.

[9]Conan Doyle, *Memories* op. cit., p. 29.

[10]See Michael Baker's essay on Charles Altamont Doyle in *The Doyle Diary* (Paddington Press, 1978), pp. v – xxix.

[11]J. Dickson Carr, *The Life of Sir Arthur Conan Doyle*, (John Murray, 1949), pp. 39 – 40 and Pierre Nordon, *Conan Doyle*, (John Murray, 1966), trans. Francis Partridge, p. 187.

[12]Conan Doyle, *Memories*, op. cit., pp. 29 – 30.

[13]A. Conan Doyle, 'The Adventure of the Reigate Squires', *Strand*, June 1893 and *The Memoirs of Sherlock Holmes*, (Newnes, 1894). Also Census, op. cit.

[14]*Medical Directory* and *Kelly's Directory for Birmingham*, 1901 – 1921.

[15]See the introductory essay by J. M. Gibson and R. L. Green (eds.) to *The Unknown Conan Doyle: Uncollected Stories*, (Secker and Warburg, 1982), p. vii.

[16]A. Conan Doyle, 'The Mystery of the Sasassa Valley'. *Chambers's Journal*, 6.9.1879 and reprinted in Gibson and Green, *Uncollected Stories*, op. cit., pp. 1 – 10.

[17]A. Conan Doyle, 'Gelsemium as a Poison', *British Medical Journal*, 20.4.1879

and quoted in J. M.Gibson and R. L. Green (eds.), *The Unknown Conan Doyle: Letters to the Press*, (Secker and Warburg, 1986), p. 13.

[18]A. E. Rodin and J. D. Key, *Medical Casebook of Dr Arthur Conan Doyle: From Practitioner to Sherlock Holmes and Beyond*, (Kreiger, 1984), p. 82.

[19]ibid., p. 82.

[20]ibid., pp. 82–83.

[21]A. Conan Doyle, 'The Sign of the Four', *Lippincott's Monthly*, February 1890 and *The Sign of Four*, (Blackett, 1890).

[22]Rodin and Key, op. cit., p. 83.

[23]A. Conan Doyle, 'The Adventure of the Yellow Face', *Strand*, February 1893 and *The Memoirs of Sherlock Holmes*, (Newnes, 1894).

[24]J. Dickson Carr, op. cit., pp. 42–54, and indications in the Conan Doyle-Hoare Family Correspondence, letter no. 6 folio 3, to Amy Hoare. This correspondence is preserved in the Berg Collection of New York Public Library.

[25]See Gibson and Green (eds.), *Uncollected Stories*, op. cit., p. xii quotes letter to Blackwood's from 'The Elms', March 1882. Also Conan Doyle—Hoare Correspondence, op. cit., undated letter from Plymouth no. 3 folio 5, Conan Doyle refers to leaving behind articles of his own at 'G. H.' (Gravelly Hill) and of owing 'Sam' (Aspinall) some shirts.

[26]*Medical Directory*, 1884.

[27]*Census*, 1881.

[28]*Medical Directory*, 1884–1905 and *Kelly's Directory for Birmingham*.

[29]A. Conan Doyle, 'Notes on a Case of Leucocythaemia', *The Lancet*, 25.3.1882.

[30]*Sunday Mercury*, 21.2.1954.

[31]Ronald Knox, *Essays in Satire*, (Sheed and Ward, 1928), pp. 98–120.

[32]Correspondence with author. And see Ronald Pearsall, *Conan Doyle: A Biographical Solution*, (Weidenfeld and Nicholson, 1977) and *Sherlock Holmes Investigates the Murder in Euston Square*, (David and Charles, 1989).

[33]G. T. Budd, *British Medical Journal*, e.g. 3.5.1879, 2.8.1879, 18.12.1880, 25.9.1880 and 20.11.1880 and see Owen Dudley Edwards, *The Quest for Sherlock Holmes*, (Mainstream, 1983), pp. 304–306.

[34]Dudley Edwards, op. cit., pp. 310–311.

[35]ibid., p. 326.

[36]*Kelly's Directory for Birmingham*, medical list for 1901. Cecil Hoare subsequently served as a surgeon in the Boer War, winning the Queen's Medal (three clasps), and settled down to be Medical Office of Health in Simonstown, South Africa. See *Medical Directory*, 1915.

[37]Dudley Edwards, op. cit., pp. 306–307.

[38]R. Ratcliff Hoare, 'Clinical Memoranda: Gout', *British Medical Journal*, 25.12.1880, and quoted in Dudley Edwards, op. cit., pp. 306–307.

[39]Dudley Edwards, op. cit., p. 234.

[40]Ronald Knox, *Literary Distractions*, (Sheed and Ward, 1958), pp. 208–209.

[41]Dudley Edwards, op. cit., p. 325.

[42]Conan Doyle-Hoare Family Correspondence, op. cit., first letter dating from 1881 and the last 1921.

[43]ibid., Conan Doyle to Josephine Hoare, postmarked 28.10.1921, no. 9 folio 5.

[44]ibid., visits indicated in the following: undated letter no. 1 folio 3; 30.11.1890, no. 7 folio 3; 15.12.1890, no. 8 folio 3; December 1890, no. 9 folio 3; September 1893, no. 1 folio 4; October 1893, no. 2 folio 4; undated, no. 2 folio 5.

[45]Obituary on Dr Hoare, *Birmingham Owl*, 1.4.1898.

[46]ibid.

[47]For David Holmes's career see *Medical Directory*, 1906.

[48]*Kelly's Directory for Birmingham*, 1884–1905, *Medical Directory*, 1906.

[49]D.S. Warren, 'Just Who Did Sell Sherlock Holmes a Violin Made by Stradivari?', *Sherlock Holmes Journal*, Winter 1982, pp. 18–19.

[50]See Chapter 5 for discussion of the Herefordshire Baskervilles.

[51]F. E. Pardoe, *John Baskerville of Birmingham: Letter Founder and Printer*, (Frederick Muller, 1975), pp. 149–152.

[52]*Birmingham Daily Argus*, 12.4.1893.

[53]Lecture tour of December 1893 in Birmingham area and stay in Aston indicated in Conan Doyle-Hoare Family Correspondence op. cit., no. 1 folio 4 and no. 2 folio 4.

[54]For conflicting versions of the fate of Baskerville's body see Pardoe, op. cit., p. 151 and *Brummagem Bugle*, February and March 1991.

[55]Pardoe, op. cit., p. 155.

[56]A. Conan Doyle, 'The Surgeon of Gaster Fell', *Chambers's Journal*, December 1890.

[57]That 'The Surgeon of Gaster Fell' may have been source of friction see Conan Doyle-Hoare Family Correspondence, op. cit., letter from December 1890, no. 9 folio 3.

[58]Conan Doyle, *Memories* op. cit., pp. 287–288.

[59]J. Dickson Carr, op. cit., p. 199.

[60]Conan Doyle, *Memories*, op. cit., pp. 287–288.

[61]A. Conan Doyle, 'How It Happened', *Strand*, September 1913.

[62]Churton Collins appears to have planted in Conan Doyle's mind the misconception that Captain Anson, Chief Constable of Staffordshire, believed that the Rev Edalji and his son George had engaged in sodomy. This allegation was to sour considerably the relations between Anson and Conan Doyle which, see Chapter 3, were destined eventually to reach breaking point. See Home Office papers eg. Anson to Home Office, 24.3.1907; Anson to Conan Doyle, 14.1.1911; Conan Doyle to Anson, 16.1.1911, and Conan Doyle's complaint to Home Office about Anson, 30.1.1911.

3

Conan Doyle and Staffordshire

As early as 1891, the year of the first serialisation of the Sherlock Holmes short stories in *The Strand*, Conan Doyle had set his fertile imagination loose on Staffordshire. *The Doings of Raffles Haw* is set in a fictional rural district, fourteen miles from Birmingham, called Tamfield, a name which may have been concocted from a combination of Tamworth and Lichfield.[1] The first name of the central character of the yarn, Raffles, was to be taken by Conan Doyle's brother-in-law, E. W. Hornung, for his famous gentleman burglar, first introduced in *The Amateur Cracksman*, a book dedicated to Conan Doyle.[2] And it would take no Sherlock Holmes to appreciate that the pronunciation of the surname of the main character in *The Doings of Raffles Haw* may have had its additional significance for the medical family Conan Doyle had stayed with in Aston.

Haw is a highly virtuous son of a family doctor. But one made rich by discovering the secret of producing gold by subjecting lead to the action of electricity. It is not simple wish-fulfilment fantasy however. Determined to use his wealth for the betterment of the world Raffles Haw finds his fine intentions disastrously misfiring. When fifteen years later Conan Doyle was to turn his attentions back to Staffordshire to tackle a real life mystery in the rural mining village of Great Wyrley it is arguable that then too the best of intentions turned somewhat awry.

The year of 1906 found Conan Doyle at the height of his literary career, widely acclaimed as the creator of the greatest detective in literature, with Holmes now having achieved world-wide fame. But the author was at a low ebb, a crisis in his life which owed something to his wife Louise having died that year at the age of 49, after a long

35

illness. She had lived some thirteen years longer than had originally been prognosticated.

Conan Doyle, whose life had hitherto been characterised by immense physical and mental energy, was overtaken by lassitude and weakness which defied medical diagnosis beyond the ascription of it to 'nerves'. He required something to shake him out of his torpor. It was fortunate timing for the case of George Edalji of Great Wyrley in Staffordshire to be brought to Conan Doyle's attention — fortunate, certainly, for George Edalji.

In his *Memories and Adventures* written nearly twenty years later Conan Doyle says he 'happened' upon a copy of the *Umpire* and read of the case.[3] But his memory may have played him falsely. George Edalji records that he sent the author a bundle of press cuttings on his case together with an appeal for help to get a pardon.[4] Edalji had by then been released on licence after serving just three years of a seven year sentence received for horse maiming. He was keen to be reinstated by the Law Society and resume practice as a solicitor.

Edalji was shrewd enough to realise he might strike lucky and win the author's confidence for his cause. People did appeal to Conan Doyle for help, no doubt feeling that if they couldn't get Sherlock on their case then his creator was the next best thing. Edalji was not to know just how timely his appeal would be.

But the case of George Edalji was to be more complex than anything Holmes would be summoned to unravel in fiction, and has been surrounded by myth largely derived from the forceful personality of Conan Doyle. An adequate treatment of this remarkably tangled case is not possible in the space of this chapter but in the following few pages we can try to distinguish some of the actualities.[5]

George Edalji was son of an Indian Parsee, Shapurji Edalji from Bombay. At the age of 14 Shapurji had been converted to Christianity, and paid for his coming to England to train for the priesthood at the age of 23 by the publication of a book *Gujerati and English*. Shapurji married a Miss Charlotte Stoneham in 1874 and became vicar of Great Wyrley in 1875, a position he retained till his death in 1918. His eldest child, George, was born at the vicarage in January 1876. A son Horace and daughter Maud were also born to the Edaljis in the years that followed.

George went on to attend Rugeley Grammar School (1887–91), during which period the first of a series of threatening letters was

St Mark's Parish Church, Great Wyrley, as it is today.

received at the vicarage and abusive messages written on vicarage buildings. That the vicarage was about 100 yards from the main road made the regular intrusion of a malevolent stranger unlikely. Use of flyleaves from vicarage books for offensive messages further suggested an insider was responsible.[6] In 1889 Elizabeth Foster, a servant maid of the Edaljis, was accused of writing the anonymous letters and graffiti directed at the Edalji family, and was bound over to keep the peace. She protested her innocence even to her death-bed which she may have been driven to prematurely by the charges preying upon her mind.[7]

In 1892 a new outbreak of mischief-making broke out at the vicarage. While George was attending Mason's College, Birmingham, a series of unpleasant hoaxes and anonymous letters visited itself on the family. In one instance a large key taken from Walsall Grammar School was left on the doorstep of the vicarage. Threats were made against the Edaljis, and bogus letters made appointments or ordered goods. Some notes even contained apologies to the one-time servant maid, Foster. Often the scurrilous missives were signed 'Yours in Satan, God Satan'.

A watch was kept on the vicarage which satisfied the police that no outsider was involved.[8] The Deputy Chief Constable of

George Edalji.

Staffordshire in April 1895 informed the Reverend Edalji that either he or his elder son or both were responsible.[9] The campaign subsided thereafter.

George duly passed his final law exam and began practising as a solicitor, with offices in Newhall Street, Birmingham. He also had to his credit a modest little book on railway law outlining in a lucid and literate way the rights of the travelling public.[10]

Early in February 1903 there began a series of animal mutilations in the area of Great Wyrley. Initially the investigation centred on those who might have a grudge against the animal owners. But about mid-June 1903 suspicion fell upon George Edalji. His habit of prowling the neighbourhood late at night, sometimes miles from the vicarage, had come to police attention, and was well attested.[11] At the end of June the police claimed they traced footprints to the vicarage from where a horse was killed, and on another occasion George had been reported seen very late at night in a field where an animal was killed.[12]

About the time Edalji came under suspicion the police began to receive anonymous letters inculpating George and others in the atrocities. The police became convinced these were written by George to mystify them and to induce them to approach him and discuss the case.[13]

Most crucially, on the morning of 18 August 1903, a red roan pit pony was found with a fifteen inch gash in its belly in a field near Great Wyrley Colliery, about half a mile from where the Edaljis lived. The police claimed they followed footprints to the boundary of the vicarage, though no casts were taken.[14] Later they secured from the vicarage items of George's clothing and anything which might have been used in connection with the outrage. Evidence in the form of George's muddy and damp clothes and some razors were taken away, and George was arrested the same day in his office in Newhall Street. Members of the Edalji family denied the police claim the clothes were wet or had animal hairs on them when found.

Between Edalji's arrest and trial in late October 1903 there was another mutilation which served to confuse matters. The police suspected some scheme by the owner to get compensation for the animal's loss.[15] This seems the reason for another animal killing in the area soon after. And in the spring of 1904 a man named Farrington was to be convicted of sheep killing in what was regarded as a copy cat crime.[16]

To further obfuscate affairs towards the end of October 1903 came the first of a very long series of letters, different in handwriting from the ones Edalji was accused of, featuring 'Captain Darby and the Great Wyrley Gang', which heaped abuse on the police, boasted involvement in perpetrating the outrages and warned of atrocities to come, including the mutilation of young women. These letters were to have a dramatic sequel in 1934 when the most industrious and persistent of all poison-pen letter writers, Enoch Knowles of

Darlaston, whose knowledge of the Great Wyrley crimes was culled from press reports, was finally brought to justice.[17]

No transcript of the trial of Edalji survives, but we have the notes of the judge, depositions of witnesses and newspaper reports, from which some picture emerges of proceedings. The contention of the campaign on behalf of Edalji was that he had not received a fair trial, and the calibre of the defence was in the years that followed much maligned. Whatever the disputability of this, one point where the proceedings were left open to serious objection was in the sudden shift in the alleged time of the crime. From the untenable accusation of doing the mutilation between 9 p.m. and 10 p.m. on the evening of the 17 August the jury was, on the fourth and last day of the trial, asked to believe Edalji went out in the early morning of the 18th to commit the atrocity.

On the face of it Edalji had a strong alibi here. The Reverend Shapurji could swear that he slept in the same room as his son, a habit of many years, with the door kept locked and the key hard to turn. The reverend was a light sleeper and would surely have heard if his son left the room, and could testify when George went to bed and when he awoke. Why this peculiar sleeping arrangement existed was not made clear.

The prosecution evidence included the various depositions of the police, and also a handwriting expert, T. H. Gurrin, who gave detailed testimony to the effect that the anonymous letters of 1903 were undoubtedly by the hand of George Edalji. The jury were shown samples of George's admitted writing and the anonymous letters and asked to decide for themselves.

The jury were convinced from all they had seen and heard, and with what degree of prejudice it is impossible to calculate now, that George was guilty. On the 23 October Edalji was convicted on the charge of animal mutilation under the Malicious Damage Act, 1861, and sentenced to seven years imprisonment.

One of the first in support of Edalji's cause after conviction was R. D. Yelverton, once Chief Justice of the Bahamas, apparently keen to uphold the honour of the solicitors' profession, who organised a petition which 10,000 signed. Another formidable ally was the Reverend Shapurji himself. Much of the groundwork in support of George's plea of innocence was done by Shapurji, encapsulated in a pamphlet published two years after his son's arrest.[18] It contained

View from the front garden of what was formerly the vicarage of Great Wyrley.

points about contradictory police testimony, and the inadequacy of the evidence of horse-hair and blood stains on George's clothes and reiterated the alibi of the locked door. He argued the importance of a Court of Criminal Appeal, so that there should be no 'cover-up' of information held by the authorities but unavailable to the accused.

The arguments and the campaign on George Edalji's behalf had some effect. But when he was finally released, in October 1906, he was not pardoned. He was still under licence for a further four years and had been struck off the roll of solicitors. This was Edalji's position when his case was first brought to the attention of Conan Doyle late in 1906.

The author met George Edalji in January 1907 in the Grand Hotel, Charing Cross. According to Conan Doyle's account: 'the first sight which I ever had of Mr George Edalji was enough to convince me of the extreme improbability of his being guilty of the crime for which he was condemned, and to suggest some at least of the reasons which had led to his being suspected'.[19] Edalji was reading a paper sideways and close to his eye, suggesting to Conan Doyle 'not only a high degree of myopia, but marked astigmatism', ruling out, the author decided, forays through country fields in the dead of night to assault animals.[20]

Conan Doyle's 18,000 word attack on the case against Edalji began in the *Daily Telegraph* on 11 January 1907.[21] Some public anticipation inevitably built up around the idea that Conan Doyle would in his investigation bring to bear the methods of his great detective hero; that here, in a real life Sherlock Holmes adventure, creator and creation would merge. A potent myth was in the making.

Conan Doyle restated many of Shapurji's arguments before the wider audience his huge reputation as the creator of Sherlock Holmes helped him command. He attacked the police evidence concerning the wetness of Edalji's coat, which given the weather late that night should have been not merely damp but sopping, the alleged bloodstains, which, said Conan Doyle, were akin more to slight gravy stains than the result of bloody animal mutilations, and the horse hairs on Edalji's coat, caused, Conan Doyle suggested, as others had before him, by the careless carrying of the coat and a piece of the horse's hide in the same bag. He also contested the flimsiness of the evidence relating to footprints. As for the chronic condition of Edalji's eyesight, an issue neglected at the trial, the accused could not possibly have negotiated his way to do the deed. Edalji, according to Conan Doyle, was 'blind as the proverbial bat, but the bat has the advantage of finding his way in the dark, which would be very difficult for him'.[22] And in any case the police were watching the vicarage on the night of the atrocity, re-emphasizing the impossibility of Edalji's guilt.

Conan Doyle imagined he had done enough to prove Edalji was innocent. But that was not sufficient. He could not rest content. He had, in the honoured Holmesian fashion, also to bring to book whom he thought the guilty party.

In 'Statement of the Case against Royden Sharp'[23], submitted to the Home Office, Conan Doyle made a series of claims against his chosen culprit. Sharp had trained in a slaughter yard and cattleship, had been absent at sea during the interregnum in the letter writing and other abuses against the Edalji family, had a long record of anonymous letter writing, in which he had collaborated with his brother, and was also responsible for acts of wanton vandalism. He had even been expelled from Walsall Grammar School, the place where the key was taken from in 1892. Furthermore, he was supposed to have shown signs of insanity on nights of the new moon. Sharp's household and bedroom were so placed that he could leave unseen at any hour of night. Conan Doyle had managed to obtain from his agents in the area what he called a horse lancet which he alleged was the weapon used for the mutilations.

To the author's annoyance the Home Office refused to act on what he laid before them. The official position was that no prima facie case existed against Sharp.[24] Captain Anson, Chief Constable for Staffordshire, was distinctly unimpressed: 'not one single scrap of real evidence has been put forward to connect the man named by Sir Arthur Conan Doyle with any of the outrages of 1903', said Anson 'nor has any single convincing reason been adduced for believing him [Royden Sharp] to have been guilty of any letter writing of a criminal nature...a great part of the statements of Sir Arthur are grossly inaccurate'.[25] Anson was obviously too intelligent to be simply cast in the role of Inspector Lestrade; why was he so sure he had 'got his man'?

Conan Doyle came to believe a major reason for the Chief Constable of Staffordshire's attitude on the question of George Edalji's guilt was racial prejudice: 'I have no doubt Captain Anson was quite honest in his dislike [of George Edalji], and unconscious of his prejudice...As I trace the course of events this dislike of their chief's filtered down until it came to infect the whole force'.[26]

On the other hand in recent years Michael Harley, as the result of researching the character of Captain Anson, became 'convinced that the thought of persecuting Edalji because of the colour of his skin would never have occurred to him'.[27] Research through Home Office papers lends substance to the view that Anson's reasons for believing Edalji guilty were somewhat more telling than racial prejudice. Though perhaps in not getting the fullest possible account of why Anson was so sure of George's guilt it might be argued that Conan Doyle's suspicions were understandable.

Horace Edalji, George's younger brother, had in 1903 communicated in confidence to the authorities that back in 1894 he had come upon solid evidence George was the originator of the anonymous letters.[28] Faced with the threat of exposure George had at that time desisted from his mischief. By the time letter writing had resumed Horace had moved away from home, working for the Inland Revenue in Ludlow. Horace vouchsafed his information because he felt an appeal on grounds his brother had not written the early anonymous letters might have put the defence on an unsound basis.[29] Horace also recorded his belief that if George did do the animal mutilations it would have been for money.[30]

Leading handwriting experts from France and the USA had also in confidential reports to the Home Office confirmed the view of Gurrin that the anonymous letters in question were attributable to Edalji, something Conan Doyle had fiercely denied.[31]

A number of Conan Doyle's other arguments were open to objection; though that these objections would not be so publicly expressed strengthened a popular conviction that the real life Sherlock Holmes was in the right. Conan Doyle, for example, exaggerated the state of the weather on the night of the crime and the extent of the bloodstains the wound would have caused. He neglected the significance of the position of the horse hairs on Edalji's clothes as reported by the examining doctor, on waistcoat and left arm, which was consistent with what might have been expected from the way the crime would have been done, rather than with Conan Doyle's theory that the hairs were rubbed off randomly as the result of the piece of animal skin being carelessly placed in the same bag as Edalji's coat.[32] Edalji's defence had suggested that the hairs had been gotten by leaning against a gate where the horse had rubbed;[33] later still George would claim the hairs were used in the manufacture of the coat.[34] According to the police the clothing had been packed in brown paper supplied by Mrs Edalji and taken to the police station in the morning. A separate visit was made to collect the sample of hide from the slaughterer's, and this was brought to the station at 6 p.m. Both pieces of evidence were medically examined that evening.[35]

Conan Doyle had asserted in the *Daily Telegraph* that there was a watch on the vicarage on the night of 17 August which, if correct, would obviously have limited George Edalji's opportunity to do what he was accused of. But about the end of July Captain Anson had decided on a withdrawal of surveillance because of the difficulties of an adequate nightly watch on the vicarage, though some watch was kept on fields nearby.[36] This restored a measure of opportunity to Edalji.

Conan Doyle's account also tends to make it appear that Edalji was rather more incapacitated by his eyesight than he was. The Home Office commissioned an eminent Wimpole Street opthalmist who concluded that Edalji could find his way quite well in an area he was

Edalji's old office premises in Newhall Street, Birmingham.

familiar with.[37] And he would be crossing fields adjoining his home where he had lived all his life. He travelled to New Street Station, Birmingham, and thence to Newhall Street, and made the return journey, every working day, and, as he admitted himself, went for walks till 9.30 p.m. at night in the Great Wyrley area (much later according to other witnesses), appearing to all intents and purposes a functioning member of society.

Understandably, Conan Doyle placed considerable importance on

Side view of the old vicarage Great Wyrley, facing the railway line, as it was in the summer of 1991.

the father's alibi for George. There was the locked bedroom door and the Reverend, a light sleeper, who awoke at 4 a.m. unable to sleep because of lumbago, his son still fast asleep three feet away. The sleeping arrangement in the household which allowed for such an alibi, the father sleeping in the same bedroom as his son while the mother slept with the daughter, is even odder when we realise there were five bedrooms in the vicarage and therefore no need for this doubling up because of space. It is quite open to conjecture that the reason for the arrangement may have been that the Reverend, knowing his son's inclination to nocturnal mischief, could by such means keep a close eye on him and stop him going out.[38] It would also be natural for the Reverend to provide an alibi for an erring son he was unwilling to offer up to the dubious mercies of the law.

In Home Office papers can be found detailed and weighty objections by Anson and others to specific Conan Doyle accusations against Sharp.[39] According to these Conan Doyle's culprit was not even in the county at the time of the most intense mischief of the 1890s, being at school in Wisbech, Lincolnshire from September 1892 to the end of

1893. Sharp had worked in his uncle's butcher's yard for a short period — not a slaughteryard. Though he served on a cattle ship from 1895 to about 1900 there was no evidence Sharp was brutal to animals beyond what the job required of him, and the ship's captain had reported him 'very good' in ability and character. Conan Doyle's evidence of wanton vandalism, the ripping of train seats, came from somebody who was himself suspected of the offence. The weapon Conan Doyle had procured was inaccurately described by the author and there was no real evidence at all it was used to mutilate animals.[40] Nor did the dates of the new moon equate with the dates of the outrages.

Conan Doyle's accusation against Royden Sharp has another flaw, pointed out by Michael Harley.[41] And that is that Sharp did not live and had never lived in Great Wyrley. Sir Arthur was vulnerable to the criticism that his sense of local geography was wanting, relying on doubtful 'agents' for his intelligence. It appears he learnt of the area at first hand from a daytrip, on 3 January 1903, on which he was obviously taken by a circuitous route to the scene of the crime.[42] Anson, going by the most direct route from the vicarage, found it 'a curiously easy walk and especially to anyone who knows the ground'.[43]

In 1903 Royden Sharp was, as Conan Doyle tells us, living with his mother, Mrs Louisa Sharp. But at Clifton Villa, Hednesford Road (now Old Hednesford Road), Cannock, just north (about a five minute walk) from the centre of Cannock, and over two miles from the site of the August 1903 mutilation as the crow flies and a lot longer and harder to reach than it would have been from the vicarage. So the point Sir Arthur makes about the ease Sharp had in leaving his home at any time of night is rather negated. The sites of the atrocities made the vicarage a likelier base of operations.[44]

Sir Arthur relied in his researches on what Harley describes as 'the Cannock version of the Baker Street Irregulars'.[45] This consisted of a miner named Beaumont, the originator of the Sharp theory, and a tea company manager called Arrowsmith. They followed Sharp about and wrote letters to him in order to get samples of his writing; Sharp kept police informed of any developments.[46] Instead of working on the spot Conan Doyle paid these agents who, no doubt intoxicated by their association with 'Sherlock Holmes', retailed much gossip and misinformation as fact. Later Beaumont was to be removed to a lunatic asylum for religious mania.[47]

Under the circumstances of George's life at the vicarage it may be thought not very surprising if he developed some unusual traits. Here was a man in his late twenties, in a family of self elected celibacy, who had slept most of his life alone in the same room as his priestly father. Some impulse to nocturnal expeditions can't be wondered at. The letters of 1892–95 suggested a neurotic disturbance associated with religion ('Yours in Satan, God Satan') and, to say the least, a highly ambiguous attitude to his father. George's larger social environment, one could imagine, had not been particularly sympathetic. Probably there had been difficulties at school because of his colour, which had led to severe identity problems. All this is speculation.

More substantial evidence as to the character of George Edalji was uncovered which was quite at odds with Conan Doyle's image of him as a 'rising young professional man'. Edalji had in 1902–03 been faced with bankruptcy which probably had its origins in a lawyer's fraud in 1900.[48] Having borrowed from moneylenders in order to stand surety for a solicitor who subsequently absconded, Edalji tried to recover his solvency through gambling on horses, on the stock exchange, and other transactions, and was being hard pressed to settle his heavy debts.[49] He made numerous appeals for funds, including one to the Birmingham M.P., J. B. Stone.[50] In a desperate state, faced with bringing disgrace on himself and his family, Edalji must have been near to mental breakdown. His arrest and imprisonment in 1903 was perhaps some relief for a young professional man on the slide.

No motive was put forward at the trial why Edalji should go out in the dead of night to mutilate animals. One pecuniary motive arising from George's financial dilemma is to be found in an anonymous letter sent to Captain Anson in 1907.[51] According to this George had become connected with men of the turf and made a fifty guinea wager with three of them in Xmas 1902 that he would maim six horses, six cows and six sheep in the rector's parish before the end of 1903. If Edalji did do all the maimings recorded in the parish till the time of his arrest then he had gone a fair way to winning his bet — for by that time five horses, three cows and some sheep had been mutilated.

Conan Doyle's generous and trusting nature at other times left him prey to the plausible dissembler, and in this case he allowed himself to be overly impressed by the professional status of George Edalji, and the chief witness for his defence, the Rev Shapurji, and, once committed to his charge, he could never allow he had been duped.

Such is the force of the views of the creator of Sherlock Holmes, reasserted in the 1920s with the publication of his *Memories and Adventures*, that writers on the Edalji case in the ensuing years continued to take Sir Arthur's own account of this bizarre, convoluted matter as sacred writ.

Conan Doyle was undoubtedly a masterful story teller. But treacherous is the temptation to transpose the rules and contrivances of detective fiction to the realm of practical crime detection. The consequence is liable to be mere 'faction'. The view that Conan Doyle was subject to this predicament was expressed in the cutting words of Captain Anson to the author, when the state of their relationship had become bitter: 'I sometimes wonder if you ever realised that the characters in this tale of yours were real live persons and could not be made to speak and move and think just as you found necessary to bring the story to its desired conclusion'.[52]

The result of the intense public campaigning on behalf of Edalji was a Committee of Enquiry which concluded that his conviction was unsatisfactory on the evidence of the trial, but that to some extent Edalji had brought the problem on himself by his authorship of the anonymous letters of 1903.[53] He was granted a free pardon, though no compensation made for his time in prison. He was also restored to the roll of solicitors, and left Great Wyrley for good to take up practice in Borough High Street, Southwark, London.

A minor Staffordshire reference which should also be mentioned here occurs in the Sherlock Holmes story 'The Adventure of the Copper Beeches'.[54] Appropriately, recalling the Edalji case, it is the story in which Holmes's famous observations about the countryside's condusiveness to crime are made. Walsall in Staffordshire is heard of in relation to a Miss Violet Hunter, who goes to consult Holmes regarding the curious conditions of her employment with Jethro Rocastle in Hampshire. She impresses Holmes and Watson, and Dr Watson evinces some disappointment that Holmes lacks further interest in her once the case Miss Hunter brought him is completed satisfactorily. Watson takes sufficient interest in the woman to follow her future fortunes and tells us at the end of the story that 'she is now the head of a private school in Walsall'.

Walsall Grammar School was the scene of some enquiries in the Edalji case in 1907 but it wouldn't be suitable for Miss Hunter's academy since 'The Adventure of the Copper Beeches' was first published in 1892. It will also be remembered that Hunter was the surname of Dr Hoare's nephew, the man who played a big role in Conan Doyle's early beginnings as a writer.

One of Conan Doyle's great friends, Jerome K. Jerome, was born in Bradford Street, Walsall, about three-quarters of a mile from Walsall Grammar School, in 1859, the same year as Conan Doyle. Jerome was a young writer in London in 1886 when Conan Doyle got to know him, the same year as Sherlock Holmes was conceived. Jerome's greatest literary success *Three Men In A Boat* appeared in 1889 — the year Conan Doyle brought Sherlock Holmes to Birmingham to solve the case of 'The Stockbroker's Clerk'.

At Conan Doyle's second wedding in September 1907, at St Margaret's, Westminster, the guests included Bram Stoker, J. M. Barrie, and figures from the West Midlands who had played a part in the author's life — Jerome K. Jerome, members of the Hoare family....and George Edalji. In that same year, what Edalji's supporters had urged was at last established, a Court of Criminal Appeal to review cases of wrongful imprisonment.

[1] A. Conan Doyle, *The Doings of Raffles Haw*, (Cassell, 1892).

[2] E. W. Hornung, *The Amateur Cracksman*, (Methuen, 1899).

[3] A. Conan Doyle, *Memories and Adventures*, (Hodder and Stoughton, 1924), p. 216.

[4] George Edalji, 'New Light on the Wyrley Gang Outrages', *Daily Express*, 7.11.1934.

[5] A full scale study of the Edalji case, the fruits of nine years of research, is promised in Michael Harley, *The Great Wyrley Mysteries: A Real Life Sherlock Holmes Adventure*, (Souvenir Press, forthcoming). Useful is the compilation by Roger Oldfield, *The Case of George Edalji*, (Staffs County Council, Education Department).

[6] *The Advertiser*, 12.1.1889.

[7] *Cannock Advertiser*, 11.3.1905, and in Home Office papers lodged in the Public Record Office, Anson to Conan Doyle, 30.12.1906.

[8] H. O. papers, P. C. Upton's report, 19.12.1892.

[9] H. O. papers, Anson's report to Home Office, 7.3.1905.

[10] George Edalji, *Railway Law For The Man In The Train*, (Wilson's Legal and Useful Handy Books, 1901).

[11] H. O. papers, statement of Anson to Home Office, 20.3.1907 and the sworn statements of Ernest Roberts, P. C. Knight, John Hart, Herbert Hughes and William Thacker.

[12]H. O. papers, Anson 20.3.1907, op. cit.

[13]H. O. papers, Confidential Memorandum on Edalji Case, (undated).

[14]H. O. papers, deposition of Inspector Campbell, October 1903.

[15]H. O. papers, Anson to Home Office, 28.12.1903, and Secretary of State's Memo to Lord Chancellor, January 1904.

[16] H.O. papers, Anson to Home Office, 25.3.1904, 31.3.1904 and 12.12.1904.

[17]*Birmingham Post*, 7.11.1934.

[18]Shapurji Edalji, A *Miscarriage of Justice: The Case of George Edalji*, (1905).

[19]A. Conan Doyle, 'The Case of Mr George Edalji. Special Investigation', *Daily Telegraph*, 11.1.1907.

[20]ibid.

[21]Conan Doyle's main articles on 'The Case of Mr George Edalji' were published in the *Daily Telegraph* on 11.1.1907 and 12.1.1907. Various responses to letters received and developments in the case were published in the papers in the months that followed and on 23.5.1907 and 24.5.1907 Conan Doyle discussed the identity of the anonymous letter writer. See also R. and M. Whittington-Egan (eds.), *The Story of Mr George Edalji*, (Grey House Books, 1985).

[22]ibid., 11.1.1907.

[23]H. O. papers, A. Conan Doyle, 'Statement of the Case against Royden Sharp', 4.4.1907.

[24]H. O. papers, Sir C. W. Mathews, D. P. P.'s office, notes and reports on Arthur Conan Doyle's case against Sharp.

[25]H. O. papers, Anson's confidential report to Joint Standing Committee, 9.10.1907, quoted also in Oldfield, op. cit.

[26]Conan Doyle, 'Special Investigation', op. cit.

[27]Michael Harley, 'An Infamous Anson?', *Staffordshire History*, Spring 1985.

[28]H. O. papers, Anson to Home Office, 22.12.1903 and 4.1.1904, and letters from Horace Edalji to Christopher Hatton, 1.12.1903, 6.12.1903 and 13.12.1903. There is some evidence that indications George was the anonymous letter writer came to the notice of the defence at his trial from sources inside the family, see Secretary of State's report of conversation with Mr. Hazell M.P. for West Bromwich who was with the Edalji defence.

[29]H. O. papers, Anson to Home Office, 17.11.1907.

[30]H. O. papers, Horace Edalji to Hatton, 13.12.1903, op. cit.

[31]H. O. papers, Alfred Gobert's reports of 13.7.1903 and January 1907, W.J. Kingsley's report of 18.5.1907 and Albert Osborn's report of 10.1.1908.

[32]H. O. papers, Secretary of State's Memo to Lord Chancellor, op. cit.

[33]H. O. papers, R. D. Yelverton, 'A Complete Analysis of the Evidence taken from the sworn depositions, together with G.E.T. Edalji's observations thereon and remarks of counsel'.

[34]George Edalji, 'Wyrley Gang Outrages', op. cit.

[35]H. O. papers, Anson, 20.3.1907, op. cit.

[36]ibid, and deposition of Inspector Campbell, op. cit.

[37]H. O. papers, Dr J. Risien Russell's report to Home Office, 2.2.1905.

[38]Clearly Anson's opinion, see H. O. papers, Anson to Conan Doyle, 28.12.1906.

[39]H. O. papers, 144/986 – 989/112737, passim.

[40]Anson believed a razor or ordinary sharp knife was used, see H. O. papers, Anson, 'Notes on Conan Doyle's Letters', 1907.

[41]Michael Harley, 'The Wyrley Maimings: Mr X Stands Accused', *Cannock Advertiser*, 18.11.1983 and *Kelly's Directory for Staffordshire*.

[42]H. O. papers, Anson to Home Office, 9.8.1907.

[43]ibid. Conan Doyle seemed to encounter a lot of obstacles which would have been circumvented going by way of the siding running along the rail line, according to Anson.

[44]H. O. papers, 144/990/112737 contains a map of the area marking the sites of atrocities.

[45]Harley, 'Wyrley Maimings', op. cit.

[46]H. O. papers, Secretary of State to Conan Doyle, 16.11.1907.

[47]H. O. papers, Anson to Conan Doyle, 14.1.1911.

[48]H. O. papers, Anson to D. P. P., 6.2.1905, and see footnotes 49 and 50.

[49]H. O. papers, Anson to Home Office, 7.3.1905, 6.1.1907 and of June 1907, quoting letter of Edalji's from jail to moneylender creditor. See also Blackwell's notes to 'The Case of George Edalji: Memoranda and Papers', and footnote 50.

[50]Letter of George Edalji to J.B. Stone, 29.12.1902 in 'Papers and Documents Relating to the Trial of George Edalji on a charge of maiming horses, 1902 – 04', part of 'A Collection of MSS Formed by Sir J. B. Stone 1894 – 1907', Birmingham Central Reference Library. H. O. papers, letter from solicitor W. G. Devon, 12.12.1907 to Home Secretary with begging letter he had received from George Edalji dated 9.1.1903, and another such dated 7.1.1903.

[51]H. O. papers, anonymous letter to Anson received 7.1.1907.

[52]H. O. papers, Anson to Conan Doyle, 14.1.1911, op. cit.

[53]Sir Arthur Wilson, J.L. Wharton and Sir Alfred De Rutzen, *Home Office Papers Relating to the Case of George Edalji*, Committee of Enquiry report, (H.M. Stationary Office, 1907).

[54]A. Conan Doyle, 'The Adventure of the Copper Beeches', *Strand*, June 1892 and *The Adventures of Sherlock Holmes*, (Newnes, 1892).

4

An Author in the Spirit World:

Some Midlands Connections

Conan Doyle evinced an interest in spiritualism while still in Birmingham. In the early part of 1880 he attended a lecture 'Does Death End All?' probably put on by a local spiritualist group.[1] His interest in supernatural matters may have been tinged with some little scepticism if a short story he wrote during his time with Dr Hoare, 'The Ghosts of Goresthorpe Grange', provides any indication. In this tale a character is cured of infatuation with the supernatural after being duped by a crook who promises to provide him with a ghost for his feudal mansion but instead drugs him and makes away with his valuables.[2]

In Conan Doyle's developing commitment to the spiritualist cause, which was to come to dominate the last decade and more of his life, the role of Birmingham-based or Birmingham-born men was to be of some significance. Two of these men were to be involved in an episode that Conan Doyle was to liken to the ramifications of a Sherlock Holmes detective story; though, as in the Edalji case, this, alas for the novelist, was once more to turn out in no way as conclusive or satisfactory as that which can be contrived through the art of detective fiction.

After leaving Birmingham for Southsea Conan Doyle began to get more drawn into psychic matters. In the later half of the 1880s he attended a series of seances arranged by General Drayson, a fellow member of the Portsmouth Literary and Scientific Society and noted astronomer and mathematician, who was convinced that the reality of life after death could be proven.[3] Conan Doyle joined the Society for

Psychical Research in 1893 but it is disputable whether he was totally decided on the reality of survival after death at the time he first met the physicist Oliver Lodge in 1902.

In 'The Adventure of the Three Garridebs' (a story with a particular Birmingham association of which more will presently be said) Sherlock Holmes is made to refuse a knighthood in 1902.[4] It happened to have been the very year Conan Doyle had, with some misgivings, accepted one. So too had Professor Oliver Lodge, a much respected physicist, who had involved himself deeply in the spiritualist movement, and in 1900 had become the first Principal of the newly chartered University of Birmingham. The two men discussed psychic matters while waiting to be admitted to the king's presence, almost to the point of forgetting why they had been summoned there that day.[5]

About the possibilities of individual survival after death Lodge was at that stage probably a more convinced believer than Conan Doyle. The degree of conviction of a man of Lodge's stature made a big impression on Conan Doyle and encouraged his eventual crusade on behalf of spiritualism. Conan Doyle was, a quarter of a century later, to dedicate his two volume *History of Spiritualism* to Sir Oliver Lodge, referring to him on the title page as 'A great leader in physical and in psychic sciences'.[6] Conan Doyle's immense respect for Lodge is abundantly evidenced in the long correspondence between the two men, preserved in the archives of the Society for Psychical Research, a correspondence which was to last right up to the year of Conan Doyle's death.[7]

Sir Oliver Lodge was born eight years before Conan Doyle, in Penkhull, Staffordshire. While working in his early years for his father in an agency for supplying materials for pottery, he had attended classes in geology and chemistry, going on to graduate at the Royal College of Science and University College, London. In 1881 he was appointed to the chair of Physics at Liverpool University where he became one of the great pioneers in wireless telegraphy. He then held his position at the University of Birmingham till 1919.[8]

Lodge had had a long involvement in spiritualism by the time he first met Conan Doyle. He had investigated thought transference as early as 1883, and in the late 1880s the claims to mediumship of a Bostonian lady, Mrs Piper. The results, published in 1890, were favourable to her powers, and convinced him of survival after death.[9]

Sir Oliver Lodge

Mrs Piper, as far as can be gathered from this distance in time, appears to have been well-versed in the technique known to stage magicians as 'muscle reading'. Often during seances she enhanced her sensitivity to psychic vibrations by placing the sitter's hand against her forehead.[10] Brandon in her study of spiritualism claims to have traced how Mrs Piper proved highly successful in her dealings with Lodge in 'fishing' for information, little clues, reactions and exclamations which enabled her to build up material on her subject.[11] Indeed her feats of 'deduction' may have had something in common with the methods of

Sherlock Holmes; they certainly impressed Lodge, who had supported also the claims to mediumistic powers of Eusabio Paladino, whose well-documented resort to trickery to achieve her ends he looked on with rather too tolerant an eye.[12] The supernatural powers of both Piper and Paladino were to be endorsed by Conan Doyle.[13]

The greatest publicity for Lodge's convictions on the subject of spiritualism came as the result of the 1st World War, in his book *Raymond, or Life and Death*. This work was inspired initially by a cryptic message resulting from a trance state of Mrs Piper sent on to Lodge in September 1915. Soon afterwards Lodge's favourite son Raymond was killed by a shell fragment near Ypres. Mrs Piper's message was deciphered with elaborate erudition as bearing upon Raymond's impending death.[14] Messages began issuing from his much beloved son from the other side, a place known as Summerland, and, defying the expected derision, Lodge went into print with the revelations. *Raymond* attempts to guide the agnostic reader to conclusions he would be least likely to embrace, including the possibility of the availability of tobacco and alcohol on the far side of the life and death divide. No matter that H. G. Wells should dismiss Summerland as 'sublimated Hampstead', the work proved an instant success with the public, going through twelve impressions by 1919 and appearing in a shortened version in 1922.[15] It struck a chord with many who also had suddenly lost loved ones in the carnage of war and, in their anguish, were seeking some tangible means of reconciling themselves to their loss.

Lodge's *Raymond* was the subject of a long and glowing review by Conan Doyle. It was, according to Conan Doyle, 'a new revelation of God's dealing with man'. 'The gap in the dark curtain has been drawn a little wider', Conan Doyle concluded, 'something unexpectedly homely and friendly is shining through'.[16] That review appeared within a month of Conan Doyle's announcement in the psychic research publication *Light* of his conversion to spiritualism.[17]

Conan Doyle had, like Lodge, suffered close personal loss in the Great War. There had been his son Kingsley, his close brother Innes and other relatives, including his wife's brother Malcolm. But family bereavement in itself is insufficient as an explanation why he was so drawn towards spiritualism after the war. His interest in psychic matters was a very long one. Nevertheless the impact of the war was profound. Such a bloody cataclysm seemed to suggest to many,

Plaque to Raymond Lodge in St George's Church, Edgbaston, Birmingham.

including Conan Doyle, that for all mankind's material progress something was badly lacking in the civilization. Out of that condemnation some might see the necessity for social and political change. For others it reinforced the need to turn away from the supposed obsession with the base materialism of modern science (even, we might say, the kind of cold calculating rationalism of a Sherlock Holmes) to forms of 'spiritual' progress; to a new religious revelation of eternal life beyond the veil of human mortality.

Undoubtedly an important contribution to Oliver Lodge's conversion to spiritualist belief was the impression made on him by the huge changes in the harnessing of the forces of nature in his years of active work in physics, from the age of steam to the beginnings of electricity. His own work on wireless telegraphy inclined him to extend the paradigm, anticipating the applicability of his discoveries to traditional religious questions and from thence to a potentially even larger revolution.[18] It was no accident just how common it was to find the use of the wireless analogy in spiritualist literature in the years which followed the major developments in that field, and it comes as no shock to learn from the fascinating correspondence between Lodge and Conan Doyle that Lodge expected results from a wireless apparatus he had rigged up for the reception of Raymond's messages from beyond the grave.[19]

Conan Doyle's approach was a more religiously-minded one than Lodge's, though influenced by the need for scientific acceptability. As Hall has observed, Darwin's *Origin of Species* was published in the year of Conan Doyle's birth and the impact of that work could not fail to be immense on the generation which followed, trying to reconcile traditional religion with the challenge presented by science.[20] In this respect spiritualism was an interesting compromise between science and religion. Spiritualism did claim to offer various sorts of visible or audible phenomena the positivist-minded scientist might accept as a form of 'scientific' argument to uphold the appealing old religious possibility of life after death; religion could be 'scientised' and faith discover a new redoubt.

For Conan Doyle between science and religion it was religion which seemed to have the final claim. He had rejected the Roman Catholicism so rigidly inculcated in his Jesuit-run public school. But religion itself he could not renounce, though he felt it should be subject to something amounting to modern proof.

Apart from Oliver Lodge, in Conan Doyle's various evangelisings for the cause of spiritualism he found some energetic allies among Midlands men. One of these, a close friend of many years, was the Birmingham-born George Vale Owen (1869 – 1931), educated at the Midland Institute and Queen's College, Birmingham, a man Conan Doyle refers to in his *History of Spiritualism* as 'so outstanding a figure in the history of modern spiritualism'.[21] Owen was a Church of England cleric who, after several curacies, had resigned to become pastor of a spiritualist church in London. Conan Doyle greatly admired Owen's narrative of the after-life derived from alleged communications from his mother and from angels, *The Life Beyond The Veil*. This book was the fruits of Owen regularly sitting himself down in his vestry after Evensong in his cassock to 'take down any thoughts which seem to come into my mind projected there by some external personality'.[22] Conan Doyle supplied an introduction to the book which demonstrates as much as anything else he wrote on the subject the extent his attitude to spiritualism was inspired by religion. 'Verily the hand of the Lord is here!' Conan Doyle told prospective readers of *The Life Beyond The Veil*. This book he described as an 'inspired document of the new revelation' is largely unreadable and unread today.[23]

Owen is the man the Professor Challenger novel *The Land of Mist* (1926) is dedicated to, and he is the model for one of the characters, the Rev Charles Mason, who performs a daring exorcism, and officiates over the wedding of Challenger's daughter to the journalist Malone. This novel provides feeble fayre beside Challenger's adventures amid the monsters of prehistory in *The Lost World*. In *The Land of Mist* the professor, originally a fierce dogmatic opponent of spiritualism, is converted to the cause after the loss of his wife, thanks to the mediumistic skills of his daughter.[24]

Oliver Lodge and another Birmingham-based man, Fred Barlow, were key figures in a curious episode in the history of spiritualism involving Conan Doyle. The Hope case, Conan Doyle was to say, became 'more intricate than any Holmes case I ever invented', though once more the real life detective did not see the case through to a satisfactory end.

At the centre of controversy were the claims of William Hope, a carpenter from Crewe, who had begun his career as a spirit photographer apparently by accident when a photo he took disclosed the image of a dead woman. Presently a 'circle' was formed in the Spiritualist Hall in Crewe dedicated to the production of similar spirit photos, impressions of the dead, known as 'extras', appearing mysteriously on both exposed and unexposed photographic plates.

There was by then nothing new in spirit photography. It had been pioneered in Mrs Piper's home town of Boston as early as 1860 by a man named Mumler who was later prosecuted for fraud. As Pearsall has said 'spirit photography gave greater openings for fraud than any other aspect of Victorian spiritualism'.[25] Deception was made simple with a little help from prepared plates or double exposures; often photographic 'extras' and existing photos bore a startling degree of verisimilitude. But such considerations did not prevent spirit photography becoming something of a Victorian fashion.

The so-called 'Crewe Circle' was a misnomer as it consisted basically of just two people, a medium named Mrs Buxton and Hope himself. Conan Doyle, an enthusiast for photography from his times in Birmingham, was impressed by the results obtained in Crewe and was to show much persistence and passion in championing Hope's

Rev Charles Mason of *The Land of Mist* as depicted in *The Strand*.

claims to authentic mediumistic powers in spite of exposures of him as a fraud. A sitting with Hope in 1917 had gone some way to convincing Conan Doyle that the man from Crewe produced 'the most important psychic evidence we have ever had in this country'.[26] Hope won an enthusiastic partisan too in the Rev George Vale Owen, who introduced the medium to influential clients.[27] One early success for the 'circle' was in persuading Archdeacon Colley, Rector of Stockton near Rugby, that Hope had produced a spirit photo of his dead mother; it was later revealed that it bore a remarkable similarity to a photo Hope had been sent to copy some years before.[28]

Sir Oliver Lodge as early as 1909 was emphatic Hope had practised deception. Lodge told readers of *Light* that in tests conducted with the Crewe Circle unexposed photographic plates, wrapped in a carefully noted manner for purposes of the experiment, had shown 'unmistakable signs of having been tampered with, carefully opened and resealed'.[29] What was more, Lodge's research laboratory at Birmingham University had been subjected to a blustering visit from Hope, who refused to give his name, seized the plate envelopes and insisted on taking them away with him so that further examination was impossible. Lodge was prompted to publish his findings to 'prevent the good nature of the Rector of Stockton and some of his friends from being imposed upon'.[30]

A confidential report to the Society for Psychical Research by the British Photographic Research Association in September and October 1920 had given it that Hope's methods were fraudulent.[31] And to Conan Doyle's lasting indignation, Hope was also impugned for fraud and sleight of hand in the *Proceedings* of the SPR by Harry Price, a magician knowledgeable in techniques of deception, an exposure recounted too in an article in the *Journal of the Society for Psychical Research* in May 1922 and subsequently in a pamphlet.[32]

Price claimed to have caught Hope substituting plates and that Hope had handed him two negatives which did not bear the secret mark specially impressed by X-rays for the experiment. Conan Doyle, who believed the evidence for Hope's powers to be 'quite final', counter accused that there had been a conspiracy against Hope, and that the wrapper of the packet showed it to have been tampered with sometime before the day of the experiment.[33] Substitution of the plates could have taken place when the packet lay for several weeks in the offices of the Society for Psychical Research.[34] In correspondence Conan Doyle attacked members of the SPR he suspected were implicated in setting Hope up, but proof was lacking.[35]

Conan Doyle wrote to the magician Harry Houdini reasserting his conviction that Hope was a 'perfectly genuine medium' and recounting a further twist to the tale:

The Hope case is more intricate than any Holmes case I ever invented. I am sure now there was trickery on the part of the investigators and that the marked plates were not in the packet when taken to the dark room. One of them was returned by post anonymously *undeveloped* to the SPR.[36]

The archives of the SPR contain a quantity of inconclusive data on the package so mysteriously returned, to an extent not possible to summarise here. In the report of one prominent member of the SPR it was suggested that the anonymous package might have been a way of confusing the more direct testimony against Hope to do with plate substitution during the experiment.[37] If so the subterfuge had some success.

It is quite conceivable there were grounds for suspecting enemies of Hope in this instance of 'exposure'. Price's integrity has come under attack since that time.[38] But Oliver Lodge, always less sanguine about the evidential value of photography anyway, restrained Conan Doyle by observing that whatever the other complications of the particular case, it cannot be taken to mean that Hope himself was not capable of fraud.[39]

Conan Doyle was fired up by what he felt was the need to see justice done to Hope. He even likened his mission to that of the Edalji case,[40] and he could not resist the promptings of the Sherlock Holmes in himself in pursuing the guilty parties: 'My pamphlet [i.e. *The Case for Spirit Photography*] is almost ready', he wrote to Houdini, 'but I hold it back in the hope of learning who the rascal was...'[41] There are no further references as to how near Conan Doyle came to laying the culprit by the heels. The reward offered by the publication *Light* for the identification of who sent the anonymous package to the SPR remained unclaimed.

Ironically enough, the creator of Sherlock Holmes had previously written to Houdini advising him to consider spiritualism 'not in the spirit [sic] of a detective approaching a suspect, but in that of a humble, religious soul, yearning for help and comfort'.[42] Advice the magician wasn't now about to take. Houdini, who had exposed other so-called spirit photographers, was convinced that Hope was a practitioner of trickery. He sent a man to Crewe specially to investigate and thereupon wrote to Conan Doyle on the exposure: 'I instructed this man to let Mr Hope and Mrs Buxton go as far as they liked. The method of manipulation, as described, is very interesting'.[43] Conan Doyle's 'faith in Hope' was to remain unshaken.

Conan Doyle (left) pictured with Harry Houdini.

Houdini was making known publicly then, what James Randi has publicised in more recent years, that whatever a man's admirable distinction in other disciplines, whether in the arts, like Conan Doyle, or in the sciences, like Oliver Lodge, he can be gulled by a lack of knowledge of the peculiar expertise known to the professional magician.[44]

In response to the 'exposure' of Hope by Price in 1922 came the book *The Case for Spirit Photography* in which Conan Doyle was critical of the SPR and supported the claims of the man from Crewe.[45] He was backed up in this by Fred Barlow of Moseley in Birmingham, the Honorary Secretary of the Society for the Study of Supernormal Pictures, Conan Doyle having assumed the mantle of Vice President.

On the subject of spirit photography Conan Doyle said of Barlow that his 'experience is so extensive as to be almost unrivalled'.[46] Barlow wrote a preface to the 1922 book and contributed a chapter in which he said that his experiments in Birmingham upheld the claims of Hope and 'that the evidence for the truth of psychic photography is overwhelming'.[47]

In his *History of Spiritualism* Conan Doyle re-affirmed his faith in Hope's 'unblemished' powers, despite 'the usual attacks from ignorance or malice to which every medium is exposed'.[48] The conviction of Hope's authenticity contributed to Conan Doyle's resignation from the SPR not long before his death. He had never forgiven the SPR for its treatment of the medium.[49]

Conan Doyle was never to know that the Hope case was to become more intricate still. For three years after his death his old ally in support of William Hope dealt perhaps the severest blow of all to the credibility of the spirit photographer.

Fred Barlow of Birmingham entirely renounced his belief in the validity of Hope's powers. 'A further ten years of careful continuous experimenting', announced Barlow 'has enabled me to say quite definitely that I was mistaken. During the whole of this period no single instance has occurred in my experience, that would in any way suggest that Hope has genuine gifts'.[50]

According to Barlow, Hope's fraudulence relied on his laying down certain 'conditions' for his 'supernormal powers' to operate, such as putting the supposedly unopened packet of photo plates in water to efface the evidence it had been steamed open. Hope's success often depended on his somehow or other getting in contact with the sensitive plate with his hands during the experiment.[51]

Tricks involved plate substitution and the furtive introduction of miniature flash light apparatus into the dark room. There was also evidence of pictures appearing in spirit photographs which had been cut out of newspapers; tell-tale photo-dots were discernible, as in the photo reproduced opposite, one example of fraud discussed in the report of Fred Barlow (pictured left) and Major Rampling-Rose (pictured

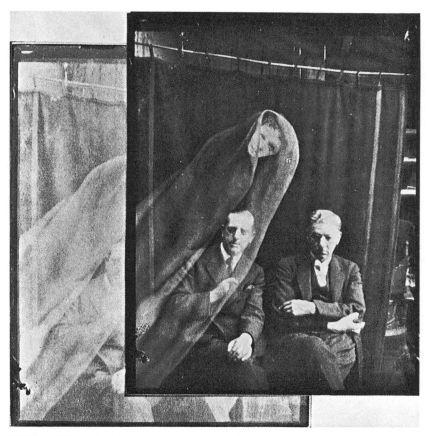

William Hope 'spirit photograph' with lightly printed original indicating double exposure — Barlow and Rampling-Rose are the sitters.

right) to the Society for Psychical Research.[52] In this particular example a lightly printed copy of the original photograph clearly betrays around the edges the give-away signs of double exposure. The pattern of the drapery, which indicates cheese-cloth or butter muslin rather than anything ectoplasmic, conceals the cut-out edges of the 'extra'. This 'extra' of Hope's bears some striking similarity to one reproduced in the pamphlet of Harry Price's exposing Hope as a fraud eleven years before.[53]

Hope's so-called 'psycho-grams', examples of handwriting appearing on unexposed plates (he even claimed samples of Conan Doyle's own posthumous writing had come through) bore characteristics of Hope's peculiar brand of literacy — or lack of it. 'Of course', said Barlow, sardonically, 'the spirits *may* have copied Hope's handwriting, grammar and bad spelling'.[54] Barlow, clinging to the possibility of genuine psychic powers, asked 'why the unpleasant task of exposing a fraudulent medium should be left to us poor mortals instead of being initiated by those on the "other side" through their genuine mediums'.[55] From the spirit world answer came there none.

Hope's spirit photography was not the only related issue Oliver Lodge was to part company with Conan Doyle on. Another notable example was the case of the Cottingley Fairies. Two little girls from Bradford claimed to have photographed fairies. Conan Doyle was quite taken with their productions, at the time managing to enlist the support of an as yet less critically minded Fred Barlow. Lodge was shown the fairy photos and annoyed Conan Doyle by expressing the view they were of American classical dancers superimposed on an English woodland background.[56] He was not far wide of the mark: they were drawings from a children's illustrated book which had been carefully supported in place by hatpins on location in the beck at Cottingley, the absence of three dimensional animation easily established today by computer enhancement techniques.[57] In old age the two ladies finally confessed their deception.[58] For many critics Conan Doyle's gullibility reached its apotheosis in the book *The Coming of the Fairies*, and could not have furnished a more obvious example of why Conan Doyle, for all his considerable qualities of mind, was no real life Sherlock Holmes.[59]

Addressing the members of the London Spiritualist Alliance in October 1931, Sir Oliver Lodge, at that time President of the Society for Psychical Research, despite his differences with Conan Doyle, was generous in his appreciation of the man:-

> His methods are not mine, he regarded himself as a missionary, a trustee of a great truth which he felt bound to share with others, whether they would receive it or whether they would reject or ridicule it, but one cannot but admire the completeness and self-sacrificing character of his life and doctrines. Occasionally, I think, he lacked the wisdom of the serpent, but the goodness of his motives must be manifest to all.[60]

Most Sherlock Holmes enthusiasts may feel a measure of relief that Conan Doyle didn't inflict a Professor Challenger type conversion upon the Baker Street detective. A sense of the need for consistency may well have restrained the messianic impulse. While the Professor was converted in *The Land of Mist* in 1926, the year of the appearance of Conan Doyle's *History of Spiritualism*, in a story first published in book form a year later, 'The Adventure of the Sussex Vampire', Holmes tells Watson: 'This agency stands flat-footed upon the ground, and there it must remain. This world is big enough for us. No ghosts need apply'.[61] Conan Doyle was never as resolute. Ghosts applied and were admitted. But in the adventures of Conan Doyle's creation, Sherlock Holmes, connected with the Midlands counties of England the arch sleuth remains firmly 'flat-footed on the ground' if maybe not always quite satisfying the most exacting standards of that detective profession he maintains to have created.

[1]K. I. Jones, *Conan Doyle and the Spirits*, (Aquarian Press, 1989), p. 37.

[2]A. Conan Doyle, 'Selecting A Ghost: The Ghosts of Goresthorpe Grange', *London Society*, Xmas 1883 and reprinted in J. M. Gibson and R. L. Green (eds.), *The Unknown Conan Doyle: Uncollected Stories*, (Secker and Warburg, 1982), pp. 129–143.

[3]G.A. Stavert, *A Study In Southsea: The Unrevealed Life Of Doctor Arthur Conan Doyle*, (Milestone, 1987), pp. 59–60.

[4]A. Conan Doyle, 'The Adventure of the Three Garridebs', *Strand*, January 1925 and *The Casebook of Sherlock Holmes*, (John Murray, 1927).

[5]A. Conan Doyle, *Memories and Adventures*, (Hodder and Stoughton, 1924), pp. 210–211.

[6]A. Conan Doyle, *The History of Spiritualism*, Volume I, (Cassell, 1926).

[7]Archives of the Society for Psychical Research, Oliver Lodge-Conan Doyle Correspondence, nos. 401–600.

[8]See Oliver Lodge, *Past Years: An Autobiography*, (Hodder and Stoughton, 1931).

[9]Oliver Lodge, *Proceedings of the Society for Psychical Research*, Vol. VI, 1889.

[10]Ruth Brandon, *The Spiritualists*, (Weidenfeld and Nicholson, 1983), p. 211.

[11]ibid., p. 210.See also J. F. Rinn, *Searchlight on Psychical Phenomena*, (Ryder, 1954), pp. 104–107, pp. 122–131 on Piper.

[12]Lodge, *Past Years*, op. cit., pp. 295–296, pp. 304–305, pp. 308–311.

[13]Conan Doyle, *History*, op. cit., Volume 2, pp. 1–20 and pp. 65–77.

[14]Oliver Lodge, *Raymond; Or Life and Death*, (Methuen, 1916), pp. 90–95.

[15]Lodge, *Raymond*, op. cit., and *Raymond Revised*, (Methuen, 1922). See also comments of Brandon, op. cit., p. 218.

[16]A. Conan Doyle, 'Survival After Death', *Observer*, 26.11.1916.

[17]A. Conan Doyle, 'A New Revelation. Spiritualism and Religion', *Light*, 4.11.1916.

[18]Lodge, *Past Years*, op. cit., pp. 333–341 and passim.

[19]Lodge-Conan Doyle Correspondence, op cit., no. 429, 26.9.1922.

[20]T.H. Hall, *Sherlock Holmes and His Creator*, (Duckworth, 1978), p. 116.

[21]Conan Doyle, *History*, op. cit., p. 220.

[22]George Vale Owen, *Life Beyond The Veil*, (Thornton-Butterworth, 1920), p. xxi.

[23]ibid., Conan Doyle's introduction, pp. xxxii–xxxiii.

[24]A. Conan Doyle, *The Land of Mist*, (Hutchinson, 1926).

[25]Ronald Pearsall, *The Table Rappers*, (Michael Joseph, 1972), p. 125.

[26]Archives of the Society for Psychical Research, File H2, Conan Doyle's evidence file to Miss Newton of the SPR, 27.7.1922.

[27]ibid, File H1, W. Price Haywood, 'Account of Seances for Spirit Photography'.

[28]Fred Barlow, 'William Hope's Photographic Mediumship', *Light*, 14.4.1933, and see also the editor's observations in *Light*, 14.2.1914.

[29]Oliver Lodge, 'Asserted Supernormal Photography', *Light*, 20.3.1909.

[30]ibid.

[31]Archives of the SPR, op. cit., File H10, Dr Higson and Dr T. Slater Price, *British Photographic Research Association Confidential Report to the SPR*, September 1920 and October 1920.

[32]Harry Price, *Journal of the Society for Psychical Research*, May 1922 and reprinted in *Cold Light On Spiritualistic Phenomena: An Experiment with the 'Crewe Circle'*, (Kegan, Paul, Trench and Trubner, 1922).

[33]A. Conan Doyle, *The Case for Spirit Photography*, (Hutchinson, 1922), passim.

[34]ibid., passim.

[35]Lodge-Conan Doyle Correspondence, op. cit., no. 455, Vol. 1924.

[36]B. M. L. Ernst and Hereward Carrington, *Houdini and Conan Doyle, The Story of a Strange Friendship*, (Hutchinson, 1933), letter from 29.10.1922 quoted p. 141.

[37]Archives of the SPR, op. cit., File H9, Mrs Henry Sidgwick's report 26.11.1922

[38]See T. H. Hall, *The Search for Harry Price*, (Duckworth, 1978) and E. J. Dingwall, Kathleen Goldney and T. H. Hall's exposure of Price's methods in *The Haunting of Borley Rectory*, (Duckworth, 1956).

[39]Lodge-Conan Doyle Correspondence, op. cit., no. 438, 20.12.1922 and no. 460, 10.6.1924.

[40]Archives of the SPR, op. cit., File H2, Conan Doyle's evidence file to Miss Newton, 27.7.1922.

[41]Ernst and Carrington, op. cit., letter from 29.10.1922 quoted p. 141.

[42]ibid., pp. 51–52.

[43]ibid., letter to Conan Doyle 8.8.1922 quoted p. 153.

[44]James Randi, *Flim-Flam*, (Prometheus, 1982) and Harry Houdini, *A Magician Among the Spirits*, (Harper, 1924).

[45]Conan Doyle, *Spirit Photography*, op. cit.

[46]ibid., p. 52.

[47]ibid., p. 70.

[48]Conan Doyle, *History*, op. cit., Volume II, pp. 144–145.

[49]For indications Conan Doyle never forgave the SPR over the Hope case see the Lodge-Conan Doyle Correspondence, op. cit., no. 439, 31.12.1922; no. 443, 2.1.1923; no. 444, 3.1.1923; no. 455, 4.1.1924; no. 483, 29.10.1924; no. 552, 10.7.1928 and also Harry Price's comments in 'Conan Doyle's Startling Message from the Beyond', *Nash's Pall Mall Magazine*, January 1931.

[50]Fred Barlow, *Light*, op. cit.

[51]ibid.

[52]Fred Barlow and Major Rampling-Rose, *Proceedings of the Society for Psychical Research*, Vol. XLI, March 1933.

[53]ibid., p. 136 and cf. Price, *Cold Light*, op. cit.

[54]Fred Barlow, *Light*, op. cit.

[55]ibid.,

[56]K. I. Jones, op. cit., p. 159.

[57]James Randi, op. cit., pp. 31–32.

[58]For the story of these confessions, Joe Cooper, *The Case of the Cottingley Fairies*, (Hale, 1990).

[59]A. Conan Doyle, *The Coming of the Fairies*, (Hodder and Stoughton, 1922).

[60]Quoted in Nandor Fodor, *Encyclopedia of Psychic Science*, (Arthurs Press, 1934), p. 106.

[61]A. Conan Doyle, 'The Adventure of the Sussex Vampire', *Strand*, January 1924 and *The Casebook of Sherlock Holmes*, (John Murray, 1927).

5

Sherlock Holmes In Herefordshire

In 'The Boscombe Valley Mystery' Sherlock Holmes summons Watson to a couple of days of adventure in Herefordshire promising 'air and scenery perfect'.[1] As with another excursion to the Midlands we will be examining, the case of the stockbroker's clerk, the doctor seems to have no great difficulty in finding a highly indulgent locum for his medical practice.

As Watson reports it, 'It was nearly four o'clock when we at last, after passing through the beautiful Stroud Valley and over the broad gleaming Severn, found ourselves at the pretty little county town of Ross'. The ferret-like Inspector Lestrade of Scotland Yard is there to meet them at the station quite convinced that their journey is a futile one and that the young man in custody, one James McCarthy, is guilty of the murder of his father, Charles McCarthy of Hatherley Farm.

John Turner, whose tenants the McCarthys are, is 'the largest landed proprietor in that part', and his daughter Alice is sure of young McCarthy's innocence. But the case against him seems overwhelming. He is seen following his father to Boscombe Pool, which lies on the boundary of Turner's private park and Hatherley Farm. A witness sees father and son arguing violently close by the pool and the young man go to strike his father. There is incriminating blood on his clothes. And the body of Mr McCarthy is found, his head beaten in by a heavy blunt weapon — such as the butt end of young McCarthy's gun, which is found in the grass nearby.

When told he is under arrest young McCarthy's reported words are '..that he was not surprised to hear it, and that it was no more than his deserts'. This remark goes against the accused when put before the coroner's jury. Holmes, on the other hand, regards it as a significant

71

"THE MAID SHOWED US THE BOOTS."

Holmes examines a clue to the Boscombe Valley murder, as illustrated in *The Strand*.

pointer to the young man's innocence, 'the signs of a healthy mind, rather than a guilty one'.

It is of incidental interest that this passage was to find some resonance when Conan Doyle a few years after this story was published assumed the 'real life' role of Sherlock Holmes to investigate the case of George Edalji in Staffordshire. On his arrest George Edalji was reported to have said: 'I am not surprised at this. I have been expecting it some time'.[2] Words also to be used at the Birmingham solicitor's trial as indications of a guilty conscience. Conan Doyle, like Holmes in 'The Boscombe Valley Mystery', believed they indicated just the reverse. But it could well be argued that such remarks might be interpreted either way — and often are. Much must surely depend on the particular way such remarks are made.

Another of the indications to Holmes of James McCarthy's

innocence can be brought into question. It has been noted that Holmes's observation that a man's height can be judged from the length of his stride does not take into account several important variables which may be involved.[3] However, we may regard this as an example where the detective does not bother Watson with more technicalities than he feels it is worth burdening him with.

Holmes has his earliest perceptions of James McCarthy's innocence confirmed, learning that he had resisted his father's eagerness to have him marry Miss Turner because of an existing wife, a barmaid from Bristol, the reason for the argument between the two men. The story hinges on a hold the older McCarthy has over James Turner from their days in Australia. Holmes has recognized the significance of the Australian dimension on the strength of an aboriginal call used by the two protagonists. The affair is brought to an apparently successful resolution, even the obstacle of the barmaid wife is disposed of, leaving Alice and James free to marry, though Lestrade is to be left empty handed.

Colonial guilt and its retribution is not an unfamiliar motif in the Holmes stories. In this particular case Turner we learn had years before been involved in armed robbery and murder. Returning to the mother country to live out his life quietly, he finds himself tracked down by Charles McCarthy, a blackmailing witness to his former deeds, an erstwhile victim, no less. The blackmailer is murdered by Turner. Holmes receives the confession of this crime knowing fate has already intervened with a verdict likely to make whatever the law might do seem superfluous. Turner is dying of some unspecified disease. Holmes, acting as the self-appointed embodiment of the law, judges the colonial guilt and its aftermath of blackmail and murder already sufficiently weighed in the balance to require no judicial settlement. Compassion is exercised so that the unsavoury exposure of guilt casts no shadow over the younger generation.

The story can be read in terms of a larger sense of guilty unease about colonial misdeeds; Holmes performs here a convincing exorcism of guilt so that a new generation, represented by Alice Turner and James McCarthy, might continue to benefit materially from the original crimes without any nagging moral dilemma being highlighted. That the unsympathetic Lestrade is to be completely defeated can only be a further source of satisfaction.

The adventure into Boscombe Valley does have the noteworthy

The first *Strand* appearance of Sherlock Holmes in a deerstalker.

distinction of marking the first appearance in *The Strand* of one of Sherlock Holmes's most famous trademarks.[4] In the story Watson refers to Holmes donning a 'close-fitting cloth cap', a phrase which had the happy fortune to be interpreted by Sidney Paget in the illustration to the tale as a deerstalker, much like the one Paget habitually wore himself. It was an inspired acquisition, suggesting hunter, tracker, poacher and gamekeeper, with perhaps just enough of a touch of aristocratic hauteur for good measure.

'The Boscombe Valley Mystery', like other of the early short stories about Sherlock Holmes, was written quickly and it would be too much to imagine it had great regard for geographical exactitude. For instance the River Severn, described by Conan Doyle as 'broad gleaming' from the train, was in fact narrow where the old line running from Paddington to Ross crossed it.[5] For the duration of their investigation Holmes and Watson take a room at the 'Hereford Arms' in Ross. There was no hotel of that name in Ross at that time.[6]

On the evening of his arrival in Ross Holmes sets off by train to Hereford Prison to interview the young McCarthy. Here we can feel more secure in speculating on locations. Almost certainly such an accused man as McCarthy would have been held at His Majesty's Prison for Herefordshire and Radnorshire in Commercial Road, just a few yards from Hereford Station, a prison built on the site of an old religious settlement, a priory dedicated to St Guthlac and now the site of Hereford Bus Station.

Boscombe Valley is described in the story as a county district not far from Ross-on-Wye. In actuality there is no Boscombe in Herefordshire, though there is one in Wiltshire, north east of Salisbury on the River Bourne, and another on the south coast of England just east of Bournemouth. Ordnance Survey maps of the Ross area haven't disclosed a Hatherley Farm either.

Many fruitless searches have been undertaken for what might provide a suitable fit for the main action of 'The Boscombe Valley Mystery'.[7] Most promising for the Sherlockian, determined on authenticity, is perhaps to be found in the parish of Goodrich, five miles south south west of Ross, in the vicinity of Hill Court. The fine seventeenth century edifice of Hill Court, seat of the Lord of the Manor of Ross, lacks the requisite red jutting pinnacles to equip it as John Turner's seat, but there is a pool nearby which can be thought of as Boscombe Pool, though it has never been called that locally. In the story Boscombe Pool is a small lake, only about fifty yards across, formed by the spreading of a stream which runs through Boscombe Valley. The pool near Hill Court is not far off being the requisite size, but the River Wye running through the valley is nobody's idea of a stream.

According to David L. Hammer the model for Hatherley Farm lies to the north of Hill Court, in the shape of Homme Farm House.[8] Just across the river, half a mile to the west from the sandstone ruin of Goodrich Castle where the poet Wordsworth met the girl who prompted the poem 'We Are Seven', once lay, according to Hammer, the original of Turner's seat. Goodrich Court, torn down in 1946, was a castellated mansion complete with the necessary towers and jutting pinnacles.[9] The interior of nearby Goodrich Church, where Dean Swift's grandfather was once vicar, preserves some of the oak panelling of Goodrich Court. Alas, none of the name of Turner ever resided at the Court as far as we can discover, it having been the seat of the Moffat family. But the immediate area does have a point in its favour that Conan Doyle was believed to have once stayed at the nearby Bishopswood estate.[10]

Donald Redmond has observed there to be a couple of Hatherleys in Gloucestershire.[11] An old moated residence called Hatherley Court

A suggested original for Boscombe Pool, in the grounds of Hill Court.

A suggested model for Hatherley Farm — Homme Farm House near Hill Court.

was situated at Down Hatherley, five miles west of Cheltenham and two miles north of Churchtown station on the Great Western Railway line. A Hatherley Brook also passes through the parish, joining the River Severn at Sandhurst. And about two miles south west of Cheltenham, some fifteen miles from Ross-on-Wye, at Up Hatherley there is a Hatherley Manor where there was also a Hatherley Inn. The two Hatherleys are now separated by a motorway junction.[12]

As early as his time in Aston Conan Doyle had written a story, 'Our Derby Sweepstakes', in which the name of Hatherley is bestowed on a house, an abbey, a church and a brook.[13] But a far better known use of the name of Hatherley is for the chief character in a Sherlock Holmes story probably written within a few weeks of 'The Boscombe Valley Mystery', 'The Adventure of the Engineer's Thumb'.[14] Victor Hatherley suffers an unfortunate amputation when called in to overhaul machinery of the counterfeiter, Colonel Lysander Stark. That adventure occurs not far from Reading, a station Holmes and Watson pass through on their way to Ross-on-Wye.

Another Herefordshire link with the subject of this chapter is that in the late 1870s Dr David Holmes was a registered medical practitioner in Hay-on-Wye, on the border of Herefordshire and Brecknockshire, twenty five miles from Ross and sixteen from Hereford.[15] Dr Holmes was to become a near neighbour of Conan Doyle's old employer Dr Hoare of Aston at about the time Sherlock Holmes was first conceived and, as we have already speculated, it is just possible that he furnished a little of the inspiration for the author's choice of the great detective's surname.[16]

A further Holmesian connection with the Welsh Marcher town of Hay, which was in more recent years to become the second-hand book capital of Britain, involves the theory that the classic Sherlock Holmes story *The Hound of the Baskervilles* may have had its genesis in the area.

A theory first advanced in the 1950s by Maurice Campbell has it that a local family legend, linked with the Vaughan family of Hergest Court, Herefordshire, about a hound whose appearances foretell the death of a member of the family — a creature known as 'the black hound of Hergest' — gave Conan Doyle the idea for *The Hound of the Baskervilles*.[17] The author learned of the legend while staying for a short period not far from Kington. In the church at Kington is to be found a magnificent tomb in alabaster in memory of two of the most

What now remains of Hergest Court.

notorious of the Vaughan family, Thomas known as 'Black Vaughan', and his wife 'Ellen the Terrible'. The Vaughan family seat at Hergest has immense importance in Welsh literature as the place where the collection of Welsh folk-tales to be translated as *The Mabinogion* were preserved.[18]

We have already suggested the possibility of a Birmingham derivation for the choice of the Baskerville name.[19] Herefordshire has its claim also, and if anything a rather weightier one. The Vaughans were neighbours of the ancient Norman family of the Baskervilles, and were on sufficiently intimate terms to have intermarried with them. The Baskervilles had long dwelt in Eardisley Castle, which was situated between Hereford and Kington but is no longer standing. Until a few years after the Second World War the Baskervilles resided in Clyro Court, about two miles from Hay, a building which now sees service as a hotel.[20] It is believed that Conan Doyle was on familiar terms with the Baskervilles.[21]

Clyro Church contains memorials to members of the Baskerville family as well as to the distinguished local diarist, the Rev Francis

Tomb of the Vaughans in Kington Church.

Kilvert. And the name of the Baskervilles is memorialised nearby too, in 'The Baskerville Arms', an inn near to the church, opposite Kilvert's old lodgings, and, appropriately, its frontage bears some debt to the suggestive Baskerville family blazon crest of a wolf's head.

However we adjudge the rival claims, there can be no arguing with the one advantage that Dartmoor retains as the most likely location for *The Hound of the Baskervilles* — and that is the telling absence of those tracts of atmospheric and forbidding moorland around Hay-on-Wye.

Worth mentioning here, as something of an addendum to Sherlock Holmes in Herefordshire, is a reference in the canon to the adjoining Midland county of Worcestershire (this is not too much of a violation of the chapter's brief given that the two old counties have since Conan Doyle's time become officially yoked together as the region of 'Hereford and Worcester').

In *The Sign of Four* we are told that Worcestershire is the birthplace of Jonathan Small, the one-legged man who has been involved in the theft of the Agra treasure in India. He survives his sentence in the Andaman Islands to return to England bent on revenge for the betrayal of himself and his confederates. In his narrative Small tells Holmes:-

79

Formerly the Baskerville residence, Clyro Court, now the Baskerville Hall Hotel.

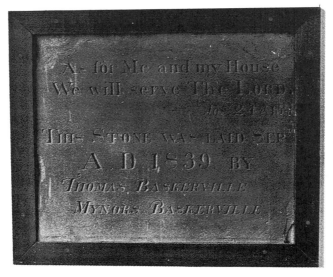

Nineteenth century plaque to a Baskerville, interior of Baskerville Hall Hotel.

Baskerville Arms, Clyro.

I am a Worcestershire man myself, born near Pershore. I dare say you would find a heap of Smalls living there now if you were to look. I have often thought of taking a look round there, but the truth is that I was never very much of a credit to the family, and I doubt if they would be very glad to see me. They were all steady, chapel-going folk,, small farmers, well-known and respected over the country-side, while I was always a bit of a rover.[22]

Pershore is a market town in the valley of Evesham on the banks of the River Avon. Research does not bear out the claim of a 'heap of Smalls' to be found in the area in the 1880s. In fact there was rather a dirth, though representatives bearing the name were to be found just to the west in Malvern and five miles to the east in Evesham.[23] Pershore was the birthplace also of the wife of the man Conan Doyle worked for in Aston, Amy Hoare.[24] And it was near to Evesham that Conan Doyle set the bizarre story of a reformed alcoholic, 'The Japanned Box', in which the area is described as 'the most English part of England'.[25]

Like 'The Boscombe Valley Mystery' *The Sign of Four* is bound up with colonial guilt and a cycle of retribution. Though in this case nobody ultimately benefits; except possibly Dr Watson, who gains for himself a wife.

[1] A. Conan Doyle, 'The Boscombe Valley Mystery', *Strand*, October 1891 and *The Adventures of Sherlock Holmes*, (Newnes, 1892).

[2] Quoted in A. Conan Doyle, 'The Case of Mr George Edalji: Special Investigation', *Daily Telegraph* 12.1.1907.

[3] A. E. Rodin and J. D. Key, *Medical Casebook of Dr Arthur Conan Doyle: From Practitioner to Sherlock Holmes and Beyond*, (Krieger, 1984), p. 212.

[4] But not strictly the first time Sherlock Holmes is depicted in a deerstalker, a distinction that the serialisation of *The Sign of Four* in the *Bristol Observer* of 1890 possesses. See J. M. Gibson and R. L. Green, *A Bibliography of Arthur Conan Doyle*, (Clarendon Press, 1983), p. 39.

[5] T. Owen and P. Porter, 'The Boscombe Valley Weekend: The Sherlock Holmes Society Summer Expedition, May 20 – 22', *Sherlock Holmes Journal*, Winter 1983, pp. 90 – 93.

[6] *Kelly's Directory for Herefordshire* 1885 – 1892.

[7] See Owen and Porter, op. cit. and D. L. Hammer, *For The Sake Of The Game*, (Gasogene Press, 1986), pp. 197 – 199.

[8] Hammer, op. cit., p. 199.

[9] ibid., p. 199.

[10] Owen and Porter, op. cit., p. 92.

[11] D. A. Redmond, *Sherlock Holmes: A Study In Sources*, (MacGill-Queen's University Press, 1982), p. 56.

[12] *Kelly's Directory for Gloucestershire*, 1885.

[13] A. Conan Doyle, 'Our Derby Sweepstakes', *London Society* May 1882 and reprinted in J. M. Gibson and R. L. Green, *The Unknown Conan Doyle: Uncollected Stories*, (Secker and Warburg, 1982), pp. 43 – 63.

[14] A. Conan Doyle, 'The Adventure of the Engineer's Thumb', *Strand*, March 1892 and *The Adventures of Sherlock Holmes*, (Newnes, 1892).

[15] *Medical Directory*, 1878.

[16] See chapter 2 'Conan Doyle and Aston'.

[17] Maurice Campbell, *The Hound of the Baskervilles: Dartmoor or Herefordshire?*, (talk given to The Sherlock Holmes Society of London, reprinted from Guy's Hospital Gazette, May 1953, by Magico, 1953).

[18] Charlotte E. Guest (trans.), *The Mabinogion: from the Llyfr coch o Hergest, and other ancient Welsh manuscripts*, 3 vols, (1849).

[19] See chapter 2 'Conan Doyle and Aston'.

[20] Campbell, op. cit., pp. 1 – 2.

[21] ibid.

[22]A. Conan Doyle, 'The Sign of the Four', *Lippincott's Monthly*, February 1890 and *The Sign of Four*, (Blackett, 1890).

[23]*Kelly's Directory for Worcestershire*, 1890–1892.

[24]*Census* 1881 gives Mrs Hoare's place of birth.

[25]A. Conan Doyle, 'The Japanned Box', *Strand*, January 1899 and in *Round The Fire Stories*, (Smith, Elder and Co. 1908).

6

Sherlock Holmes In Derbyshire

'The Adventure of the Priory School' takes Sherlock Holmes and Dr Watson to 'Mackleton' in the Peak District.[1] This excursion is prompted by a visit to Baker Street by a Dr Thorneycroft Huxtable, who tells of the abduction of a pupil of illustrious birth from 'the most select preparatory school in England' situated near 'Mackleton', which Dr Huxtable owns and runs. The victim is Lord Saltire son of the Duke of Holdernesse 'one of the greatest subjects of the crown'. Both the boy and a German master have vanished, with the presumption being that the master is responsible for the kidnapping.

Holmes's on the spot investigation of the case uncovers a murder, not that of the abductee but of the German master initially suspected of the abduction. In tracking the bicycle tyre marks of the boy and master across the moors the German master is found. Holmes is eventually able to uncover the plot of the illegitimate son of the duke, James Wilder, who doubles as the duke's secretary, to abduct the young Lord Saltire with the aim of forcing the duke to change his will. The plan has gone appallingly wrong because the man Wilder engaged as an accomplice, Reuben Hayes, landlord of the Fighting Cock Inn, has fatally wounded the German master who had set off in the boy's pursuit. The boy, lured out by the prospect of a meeting with his mother, had been held at the inn by Hayes.

A couple of minor flaws in the story are often remarked by critics, and do serve to make the tale not as wholly convincing an example of the art of the detective story as it might otherwise be.

The first concerns Holmes's tracking of the bicycle tyre marks across the moor. Rather a surfeit of ink has already been expended on those tyre tracks to warrant much further comment here.[2]

85

Readers of the story in *The Strand*, on the alert to out-detect the detective, wrote in to explain that Holmes's observation that the tyre tracks could indicate the direction the parties travelled in was without foundation. Conan Doyle tells us in his *Memories and Adventures* that he received 'many remonstrances upon this point, varying from pity to anger', and he acknowledges his readers were correct, but also records a felicitous escape clause to justify the detective and leave his reputation intact: it is possible to know which way a bicycle is going should it be travelling over uneven ground such as undulating moorland.[3] That this is not fully made clear in the tale must be accounted a flaw, albeit a rather minor one. It is easy to excuse the omission on the basis that Holmes, who we are told is able to recognize forty-two different impressions left by tyre marks, would likely have kept back from Watson the full extent of his grasp of the evidence in the heat of the hunt.

Another much noted minor flaw relates to Holmes's suggestion that the duke can convince the rascal Hayes, who is sure to hang, that it is in his interests to keep silent. Meanwhile the duke's bastard son Wilder will disappear off to Australia to begin life anew. If a man is due to hang, especially one as unscrupulous as Hayes, who we already know has a grudge against the duke, it is difficult to see just what further interest he stands to lose; particularly when he comes to realise the plain injustice that the prime mover in the misadventure is going to entirely escape the clutches of the law. Indeed by accepting payment from the duke and failing to reveal the full circumstances of the crime to the police, Holmes may be held to have implicated himself rather badly.

Just where the fictional 'Mackleton' is supposed to be has been the subject of speculation over the years. Harrison has suggested it is a composite of the names of Matlock, some ten miles from Chesterfield, and Alfreton, some eleven miles from Chesterfield.[4] Quite ingeniously, it has been advanced, by Bernard Davies in his tour de force of research on the case, that the action of the story takes place north east of Matlock and that 'Mackleton' is therefore an anagram of N. E. Matlock.[5] Philip Weller has concluded that 'Mackleton' combines something of the area of Matlock and Castleton, with the station referred to in the story being Darley Dale.[6] Less convincingly, Macclesfield in Cheshire has also been put forward.[7] It is evident from Conan Doyle's original manuscript, available in

Holmes and Watson tracking tyremarks across the moors — illustration from *The Strand*.

facsimile, that he himself originally had Castleton in Derbyshire in mind before he decided on an invented place name.[8]

Well-known features of the area around Castleton are the old mine workings where the world famous Blue John stone was extracted,

87

Holmes and Watson approach the Fighting Cock Inn — illustration from *The Strand.*

much prized by Victorians. It was this terrain which was to provide Conan Doyle with the setting for another piece of fiction, a masterful horror tale, appearing six years after 'The Adventure of the Priory School'. Not far from the town of Castleton Dr James Hardcastle was to encounter 'The Terror of Blue John Gap'.[9] a fearsome bear-like monster inhabiting the bowels of the earth, invoked by the author, it would seem, at about the time he was suffering a severe bowel disorder.[10] This might lead one to conclude it was dwelling on internal rather than external landscape which provided the major inspiration.

In using the name of 'Hallamshire' instead of Derbyshire in 'The Adventure of the Priory School' Conan Doyle was aware that Hallamshire was an ancient lordship whose boundaries straddle both Yorkshire and Derbyshire. The name of Hallam Moors still survives in the north of Derbyshire as does West Hallam just west of Ilkeston with Kirk Hallam situated nearby. Sheffield was the principal town of the ancient Saxon manor of Hallam; it is not too much to suggest that the young Conan Doyle may have begun to familiarize himself with the area in which 'The Adventure of the Priory School' takes place during his short stay as a medical dispensary assistant to Dr Richardson in the town of Sheffield. A respite in or around that time in the ruggedly picturesque area of the Peak District might have come as some sweet relief from a less than happy few weeks in the cutlery town. His mother had moved to the West Riding of Yorkshire after the committal of her husband to an asylum in Dumfries, and we know Conan Doyle visited her there not long after he acquired his ill-fated motor car, and shortly before he wrote 'The Adventure of the Priory School', and would have renewed familiarity with the Peak District then.[11]

It has been asked why in the story the great detective is made to refer to Derbyshire as the 'North of England' when the county is always thought of as being very much of the Midlands. This might be attributed to metropolitan bias. But the Peak District is from the simple descriptive viewpoint certainly geographically well north of the centre of England. And we may recall that Holmes does refer to the county of Herefordshire in 'The Boscombe Valley Mystery' as the 'West of England'. Additionally Conan Doyle, as we have suggested, may have associated the Peak District with his time in Sheffield, a town just over the border in Yorkshire, and also later with his visits to his mother in the West Riding. Yorkshire is a county which is always bound to be thought of as an integral part of the 'North of England'.

It is of some passing interest that the man who played a large part in encouraging Conan Doyle to a literary career when the young medical

The 8th Duke of Devonshire.

student was working for Dr Hoare in Aston, Rupert Hoare Hunter, had strong connections with the area of Derbyshire, having been assistant surgeon at Belper Union Infirmary and assistant physician at the Matlock House Hydropathic Company Limited in Matlock, a lavish and substantial example of many such establishments which developed in the spa town in the nineteenth century to administer to the health craze of Victorians convinced of the restorative nature of local mineral waters.[12]

Speculation has inevitably been applied to the real-life identity of the character the 'sixth Duke of Holdernesse', referred to in 'The

Suggested models for Holdernesse Hall — Haddon Hall

and Chatsworth House.

Adventure of the Priory School' as 'the late Cabinet Minister'. He is a man, according to Holmes's 'encyclopaedia of reference', loaded down to the gunnels with titles: Baron Beverley, Earl of Carston and Lord Lieutenant of Hallamshire since 1900, owner of about 250 acres of

91

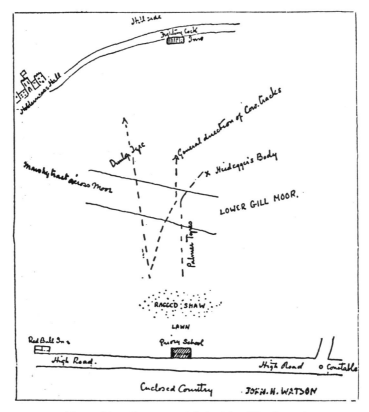

Map of locality, as published in *The Strand.*

land, with addresses given as Carlton House Terrace; Holdernesse Hall, Hallamshire and Carston Castle, Bangor, Wales. He was Lord of the Admiralty, 1872 and Chief Secretary of State for something or somewhere Holmes never gets around to stating. No wonder Holdernesse is referred to as 'one of the greatest subjects of the crown'.

Harrison likens the Duke of Holdernesse to the Duke of Norfolk, who owned land around Sheffield.[13] But if there is a prototype one would have to strongly incline, as most commentators do, to Spencer Compton Cavendish, the 8th Duke of Devonshire (1833 – 1908), who had indeed been 'the late Cabinet Minister', under Balfour at the time the story was being written. With Cavendish the fictional 'Duke of

Stancliffe House, suggested as the original for 'The Priory School'.

Holdernesse' had a compelling list of career correspondences. The 8th Duke had been a Lord of the Admiralty in 1863, Secretary of State for War in 1866, Chief Secretary of State for Ireland 1870–1874 and Secretary of State for India.[14] One other, less august position would not have escaped Conan Doyle's sometime attention. Cavendish was Lord Rector of the University of Edinburgh in 1879 at a time when as a young student Conan Doyle was still attached to the University Medical School.

If the theory as to the Duke of Holdernesse's identity is correct then either Chatsworth House or Hardwick Hall, both owned by the Duke of Devonshire, bulk large as likely originals of Holdernesse Hall. Haddon Hall also has had its supporters. Though owned by the Duke of Rutland and vacant at the time of the adventure involving the Priory School, it seems possible Conan Doyle included in the story some architectural features from that source.[15]

A few years ago Bernard Davies, elaborating the original map of the locality which had been published in *The Strand*, fixed in his search for locations upon an area just north east of Matlock, identifying Holdernesse Hall as Chatsworth House and Lower Gill Moor, the scene of the moorland adventures of the tale, as East Moor.[16] This has

The Highwayman as it was in the summer of 1991.

found support from Philip Weller, who feels he has located the original Priory School as Stancliffe Hall in Darley Dale.[17] Stancliffe had strong connections with Chatsworth House, and Weller has discovered the rather appealing fact that the incumbent of Stancliffe till 1887, the distinguished engineer, Sir Joseph Whitworth, had a legal dispute with a neighbour by the name of Holmes. Stancliffe did become a boy's preparatory school soon after Whitworth's death. Being about six miles from Chatsworth, it is seen by Weller as the ideal location for the education of the Duke of Holdernesse's son.[18]

Davies and Weller concur that the original of the 'Fighting Cock Inn' is the Highwayman, once known as the New Inn, standing on the

Plaque on Revolution House, Old Whittington.

Baslow to Chesterfield road.[19] It is not the 'forbidding and squalid inn' described in the story, at least not today. Though Davies speculates that as a consequence of the advent of the railway it may have been reduced to such a status by the turn of the century.[20]

One Sherlockian has entertained the idea that the original for Hayes's 'Fighting Cock Inn' is The Revolution House in Old Whittington, on the high road and about four miles from Chesterfield.[21] A likely point in its favour is that it bears a plaque upon it which informs us that on the site the Earl of Derbyshire, Earl of Devonshire and Mr John D'Arcy, eldest son of the Earl of Holderness, met sometime in 1688 to orchestrate measures which led to the revolution of that year.

Whether or not The Revolution House is to be regarded as the model for the 'Fighting Cook Inn' it is of historical interest and of some relevance to our case. The earldom of Holderness (note the absent last e) became extinct in the eighteenth century and it is quite possible that the memorial, or at least knowledge of the particular historical association of the Earl of Devonshire, later the 1st Duke of Devonshire, and the son of the Earl of Holderness, as co-conspirators

95

The Duke of Holdernesse with his illegitimate son, as illustrated in *The Strand*.

against the Catholic James II, suggested to Conan Doyle the substitution of the name of the Duke of Holdernesse for that of the 8th Duke of Devonshire. Holderness, a peninsula in the East Riding of Yorkshire, contains the market town of Beverley, and we recall Conan Doyle confers on his fictional duke, among other titles, that of 'Baron Beverley'.[22] We can be sure that such allusions would not have been lost on the 8th Duke of Devonshire.

More important than his other claims to distinction, the Duke of Devonshire would have commanded Conan Doyle's attention as a foremost advocate of free trade policies, engaging in dispute his successor as Liberal Unionist leader, Joseph Chamberlain of Birmingham, an advocate of a system of Imperial preference. Devonshire incurred the resentment of protectionists, who were inclined to interpret his ambiguity of behaviour as duplicity.[23] Devonshire had resigned as head of the Privy Council in the Balfour cabinet over the tariff question in October 1903, so was a highly topical figure to feature as the model for the duke in 'The Adventure of the Priory School', a story published in early 1904.[24]

Conan Doyle was himself a Liberal Unionist, and in the early years of the century was an energetic supporter of the protectionist policies advanced by Chamberlain. This commitment was expressed in meetings, articles and letters to the press, which included, for example, arguing for protection for the woollen industries of Yorkshire and the Border Burghs of Scotland.[25]

It was thanks to the urgings of his old friend Joseph Chamberlain that Conan Doyle was to stand for Parliament in the 1906 General Election as a Liberal Unionist candidate, with protectionist policies an important part of his election platform.[26] Had he not been badly beaten in the constituency of the Border Burghs of Hawick, Selkirk and Galashiels it is entirely likely the Edalji case would never have engaged his attention to the extent that it did and it is even possible that his last years would have been dominated by politics rather than spiritualism.

It is surely some indication of Conan Doyle's sense of humour at work that a thinly disguised character who can be readily identified as a political opponent at a time when the author was extremely interested in politics is eventually found to be implicated in a clandestine love affair and scandalous conduct in regard to his legitimate son.

It adds some further substance to the argument when we learn that the 8th Duke had sown his share of wild oats, having had as a mistress for thirty years the Duke of Manchester's wife and having had an affair with a courtesan by the name of Walters. As far as can be ascertained no illegitimate children resulted. But neither relationship seems to have been much of a secret.[27]

All in all it is not so very surprising that, when they meet face to face at the close of the Priory School adventure Holmes is made to show little in the way of deference to the duke's position. He upbraids him fiercely for condoning a felony, for helping the escape of a murderer, and in so doing colluding in the further detention of his younger son, to the extent that the duke is quite taken aback: 'The proud lord of Holdernesse was not accustomed to be so rated in his own ducal hall. The blood flushed into his high forehead, but his conscience held him dumb'.

Not so very surprising either that 'The Adventure of the Priory School' has at its conclusion Sherlock Holmes, the amateur detective, whose source of income to support himself is often so obscure, pocketing with some alacrity a very large cheque from the duke for services rendered. If the model for the character was the Duke of Devonshire he could well afford to pay, with a rent-roll then of about £200,000, not to mention the riches he had amassed in the various houses he owned.

As we also see in the next chapter, Conan Doyle was not above the employing of jokes in his Holmes stories. In this instance, in exposing the weaknesses of a fictional duke, it is a joke which anyone aware of the politics of the time, and of Conan Doyle's small part in them, is likely to have instantly recognized. One might imagine the Duke of Devonshire, who could hardly have been unaware of the author's disapproval of his politics, less than best pleased were he to pick up a copy of *The Strand* and discover just what extraordinary form such antipathy could take.

Before leaving Derbyshire we should record one other Holmesian association with the county (we need not be detained by the reference in *The Valley of Fear* to Derby as one of twenty places where the Birlstone murderer has been sighted).[28] It was at Chesterfield that Neville St Clair, 'The Man With The Twisted Lip', went to school and where his father was a schoolmaster.[29] Maybe St Clair's would not have been select enough a background to equip him for entry into Dr Huxtable's Priory School academy, where his talents for acting unsavoury roles might have made him an unpopular pupil with the pompous, dignified principal. If Dr Huxtable's establishment represented aristocratic pretension (and its actuality) St Clair's life-style represented the nouveau-riche; an unlikely enough entrepreneurial success story was to be his lot, a character whose wealth was to accrue from perfecting the art of professional beggary.

Neville St Clair in his alias Hugh Boone, 'The Man With The Twisted Lip', as depicted by Sidney Paget in *The Strand*.

[1] A. Conan Doyle, 'The Adventure of the Priory School', *Collier's*, January 1904, *Strand*, February 1904 and *The Return of Sherlock Holmes*, (Newnes, 1905).

[2] e.g. Dr Kohti Naganuma, 'On Tyres in "The Priory School"', *Baker Street Journal*, June 1965; T. D. Stowe, 'More About Tyres in "The Priory School"', *Baker Street Journal*, December 1965; Peter Coleman, 'Sherlock Holmes and the Bicycle', *The Priory School Contract*, (The Franco-Midland Hardware Company Annual Report, 1990); Alan Saunders, 'On the Direction of Cyclists', *The Priory School Contract Reviewed*, (The Franco-Midland Hardware Company Interim Report, 1990).

[3] A. Conan Doyle, *Memories and Adventures*, (Hodder and Stoughton, 1924), p. 107.

[4] Michael Harrison, *In The Footsteps of Sherlock Holmes*, (Cassell, 1958), p. 270.

[5] Bernard Davies, *A Ramble Through The Ragged Shaw*, (Sherlock Holmes Society of London, 1985), p. 29.

[6] Philip Weller, 'The Geography of the Priory School', *The Priory School Contract*, op. cit., pp. 5 – 9.

[7] M.S. Berdan, 'The Great Derbyshire Duke-out', *Baker Street Journal*, June 1989.

[8] A. Conan Doyle, 'The Adventure of the Priory School', facsimile of the original manuscript, with an introduction by Len Deighton, (Santa Teresa Press, 1985).

[9] A. Conan Doyle, 'The Terror of Blue John Gap', *Strand*, August 1910 and *The Last Galley*, (Smith, Elder and Co, 1911).

[10] Charles Higham, *The Adventures of Conan Doyle*, (Hamish Hamilton, 1976), p. 66.

[11] ibid., p. 181.

[12] *Medical Directory*, 1905.

[13] Harrison, op. cit., p. 69.

[14] *Dictionary of National Biography*, Second Supplement, Volume 1, 1912, pp. 323 – 329. And Davies, op. cit., p. 51.

[15] Weller, op. cit., p. 9.

[16] Davies, op. cit., p. 23.

[17] Weller, op. cit., p. 8.

[18] ibid., p. 8.

[19] Davies, op. cit., pp. 23 – 25, Weller, op. cit., p. 9.

[20] Davies, op. cit., pp. 23 – 24.

[21] C. O. Merriman, *Baker Street Journal*, December 1962.

[22] Davies, op. cit., pp. 41 – 42, Christopher Wills-Wood, 'The Sixth Duke of Holdernesse', *The Priory School Contract*, op. cit., p. 20.

[23] Julian Amery, *Joseph Chamberlain and the Tariff Reform Campaign*, Volume

5 of *The Life of Joseph Chamberlain*, (MacMillan, 1969), p. 374.

[24]Bernard Holland, *Life of The Duke of Devonshire*, (Longmans, 1911), Volume 2, pp. 305–371.

[25]A. Conan Doyle in *The Times*. 31.10.1903, 7.11.1903, *The Spectator*, 4.6.1903, 18.7.1903 and also see his pamphlet *The Fiscal Question*, (Henderson, 1905).

[26]On the 1906 election see Conan Doyle, *Memories*, op. cit., pp. 205–207.

[27]Davies, op. cit., pp. 61–62.

[28]A. Conan Doyle, *The Valley of Fear, Strand*, 1914–15, (Smith, Elder and Co, 1915). Other Midland towns mentioned for sightings of the Birlstone murderer are Derby, Leicester and Nottingham. Further minor Doylean interest in Derbyshire is furnished by the author's interest in a murder which took place about four miles from Matlock in the early 1860s, when a deranged suitor named Townley murdered the object of his affections, a case discussed by Conan Doyle in *The Strand*, April 1901, the second of a short series entitled 'Strange Studies From Life'.

[29]A. Conan Doyle, 'The Man With The Twisted Lip', *Strand*, December 1891 and *The Adventures of Sherlock Holmes*, (Newnes, 1892). Another character from the Holmes tales with some claim to Midlands' schooling is the ill-fated Willoughby Smith of 'The Golden Pince-nez', *Strand*, July 1904 and *The Return of Sherlock Holmes*, (Newnes, 1905), who was educated at Uppingham Public School, now in Leicestershire, but in the county of Rutland in Conan Doyle's time. Uppingham was the school attended by Conan Doyle's brother-in-law and creator of Raffles, 'the amateur cracksman', E. W. Hornung.

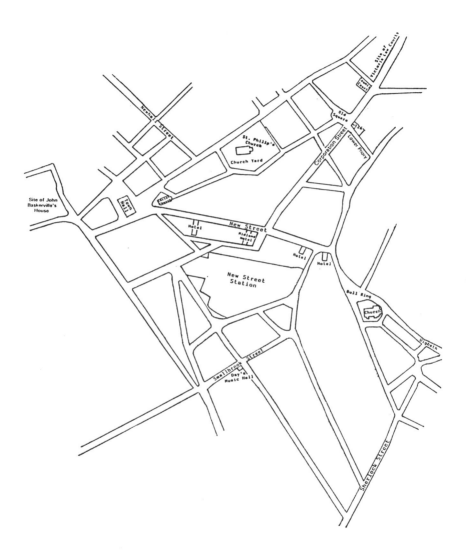

Simplified map of central Birmingham c. 1890
indicating places of relevance.

7

Sherlock Holmes In Warwickshire

During Conan Doyle's time the county of Warwickshire embraced both Birmingham and Coventry, which were that county's principal centres of population. In recent years both have been officially consigned to a region called the West Midlands, but at the time of writing it is likely their position as part of Warwickshire will yet be restored.

Birmingham and Coventry are referred to in the Sherlock Holmes tales, though the detective's links with the latter town must be conceded to be rather tenuous. The couple of minor references to Coventry in the stories do have at least one point in common, however — and that is bicycles, as most befits a place which was known as the home of cycling.

In 'The Five Orange Pips', set in 1887, we hear of Coventry as the place where Joseph Openshaw had a small factory he was able to adapt and expand with the advent of the bicycle.[1] Here we learn he patented the 'Openshaw unbreakable tyre' and made his fortune. A keen cyclist himself, Conan Doyle would have been aware of Coventry as the major centre for bicycle manufacturing in Britain up to and including the 1880s. Small firms had early on flourished there which, like Openshaw, were to prove very adaptable to the new demand for bikes. The Midlands cycle business had had its basis in craftsmen who had acquired their skills in the sewing machine industry and related trades — though there were examples of adaptation too from umbrella and watch making.[2]

There is no record of the specific unbreakable tyre referred to in 'The Five Orange Pips' and there is no indication in the text just what the nature of this wonder tyre might have been. From Coventry in the

103

early 1870s had come the first round rubber tyre. Being of solid rubber construction the likes of this could, with the hyperbole of advertising licence, be marketed as 'unbreakable'.[3] But whatever the Openshaw innovation it would not have anticipated the kind of technological developments imminent in 1887. By the time the story is set in a new 'safety' bicycle was about to usher in a new popularity to cycling, being, as its name indicates, safer than the 'ordinary' or penny farthing bone-shaker.[4] And a year after the fictional events of 'The Five Orange Pips' the revolutionary Dunlop pneumatic tyre, which was to feature in patched form in 'The Adventure of the Priory School', made its appearance upon the scene.[5] By the 1890s solid tyred bikes were to be quite out of vogue and Birmingham was about to replace Coventry as the leading bicycle manufacturing centre in the country.[6]

Whether or not like Holmes Conan Doyle was 'familiar with forty-two different impressions left by tyres', he was, before being smitten by the motor car mania, an enthusiastic cyclist, and in the course of riding he claimed to have thought up ideas for his stories.[7]

As in *The Valley of Fear* in 'The Five Orange Pips' a colonial nemesis in the form of an American secret society visits itself on a family, overtaking the bicycle entrepreneur Joseph and then his son, John, who had gone to Sherlock Holmes for help. Any theory that the story is a parable about the rising competition from the USA felt by the British cycle industry might be regarded as far-fetched. But, however interpreted, the case cannot be reckoned one of Holmes's most successful endeavours. Watson reports Holmes as being 'more depressed and shaken than I have ever seen him'. The loss of a client must always be considered bad for business.

Considerably more fortunate is Cyril Morton in 'The Adventure of the Solitary Cyclist', first heard of as an electrical engineer and employee of the Midland Electric Company in Coventry.[8] In the year the story appeared (1904) there was no Midland Electric Company in the town. There was a Coventry Corporation Electric Light Department in Sandy Lane but the Midland Electric Light and Power Company Limited was located in Wise Street, Leamington Spa, six miles away, where indeed it was still to be found in the year the story is set.[9]

Young Morton is engaged to the beautiful Miss Violet Smith who goes to Holmes worried because she is being followed by a solitary

Conan Doyle, with his first wife, on his tricycle.

cyclist every time she rides out from the Surrey house where she is employed as a music teacher. By the end of the story Morton's and Miss Smith's fortunes are transformed, thanks to the familiar device of the hidden will, and Cyril becomes a senior partner in a famous firm of Westminster electricians.

Conan Doyle uses Birmingham in a significant way in two of his Sherlock Holmes stories, in 'The Adventure of the Stockbroker's Clerk' and 'The Adventure of the Three Garridebs'. Two other passing references to the city are not without some interest.

'The Adventure of the Three Gables' contains a reference to Birmingham as a false alibi of a black pugilist called Steve Dixie, who has the audacity to burst into the detective's rooms in Baker Street like a 'mad bull' to try to warn Holmes off the pursuit of an investigation.[10] Dixie claims to be training in the Bull Ring, Birmingham at the time of a killing outside Holborn Bar, but Holmes knows better and thus gains the advantage over the bruiser without the need for recourse to violence.

The Bull Ring derived its name from an iron ring, once situated in front of a row of butcher's shops there, used to tether down the bull before it was slaughtered. It is a traditional market area in the heart of Birmingham long associated with a variety of popular culture and entertainment.[11]

While in Birmingham Conan Doyle would have heard the old stories of the bare-knuckle prize-fight culture, which by then was already in sore decline thanks to the attentions of the police authorities. Since the withdrawal of support from prize-fighting by the aristocratic 'Fancy' it had become heavily penetrated by the criminal classes.

But not many years before Conan Doyle's sojourns in Aston, just a few yards down from the Bull Ring, in Digbeth, the legendary 'White Lion' boxer's public house had prospered under the ownership of Bob Brettle, who held to his credit a victory over the redoubtable Jem Mace, one of the greatest world champions of prize-fighting history. Sporting houses which attracted followers of boxing were still in existence in the town centre in Conan Doyle's time. And in Conan Doyle's poem 'Bendy's Sermon', about a Nottingham prize-fighter turned bible-basher, Bendigo, who comes to preach at Ebenezer Chapel, Birmingham, numbered among the bruisers intent on breaking Bendy's sermon up is one 'Connor from the Bull Ring'.[12] Connor it was who 'had all that he could do/Rakin' for his ivories that lay about the pew'. That poem was obviously based on one of the

Steve Dixie accosts Holmes — illustration from *The Strand*.

stories Conan Doyle was told about the old prize-fighting days in Birmingham.

Black pugilists like Steve Dixie were not at all unusual. The invasion of black Americans into British prize-fighting circles began in the early nineteenth century, the most well-known representative being Tom Molineaux, famed for his battles with Tom Cribb (prints of both of these pugilists, incidentally, graced the bedroom wall of Conan Doyle's home in Windlesham at the time of his death).[13]

Holmes could afford to be fearless in facing down Dixie, not merely because of the information he had over him but because of his own considerable pugilistic abilities suitably evidenced in other adventures. It will be remembered that Conan Doyle used boxing in a number of his non-Holmes stories too.[14] Most memorably he captured the era of the Regency prize-fighting culture in *Rodney Stone*.[15] Conan Doyle was an accomplished and enthusiastic amateur heavyweight himself, and sufficiently respected in professional boxing circles to have been invited to referee the controversial Johnson-Jeffries World Heavyweight Championship fight of 1910.[16]

In 'The "Gloria Scott"' (published in *The Strand* the month after 'The Adventure of the Stockbroker's Clerk'), a case set when Holmes is still at college, a sister of a student friend, whose father has a dreadful secret, dies of diphtheria in Birmingham.[17] Maybe Conan Doyle was recalling the epidemics that he knew had afflicted Aston in the period. At that time diphtheria was a highly infectious killer, especially among children, with death usually occurring after a harrowing, drawn-out illness. The bacillus for diphtheria was isolated only in 1884, three years after Conan Doyle left Dr Hoare's practice in Aston, when he was still working as a doctor in Southsea; and it would seem that Professor Joseph Bell of Edinburgh, who Conan Doyle was to claim played such a part in the construction of the figure of Sherlock Holmes, was a survivor of the disease.[18] Since about 1940 a policy of general immunisation with diphtheria toxoid has resulted in the virtual eradication of the disease in the areas covered by it.

In both 'The Adventure of the Stockbroker's Clerk' and 'The Adventure of the Three Garridebs' a character is dispatched to Birmingham as a major diversion which enables misdeeds to be committed in his absence.

'The Adventure of the Stockbroker's Clerk' brings Holmes and Watson to Corporation Street, Birmingham.[19] The clerk of the tale,

Hall Pycroft, has been lured away from his rich stockbroking firm in Lombard Street to a Birmingham office by self-styled 'financial agent' Arthur Pinner, in the expectation of a money-spinning appointment as a manager of something called the 'Franco-Midland Hardware Company Limited' which boasts 'one hundred and thirty-four branches in France, not counting one in Brussels and one in San Remo'. Pycroft's resulting suspicions about this institution are confided to Holmes, who, together with Watson, come for the day to the city to personally interview the rather doubtful Mr Harry Pinner, supposedly the brother of the financial agent, in his offices at I26B Corporation Street.

126B is described by Pycroft as 'a passage between two large shops which led to a winding stone stair, from which there were many flats, let as offices to companies of professional men' — one of the suspicions excited in Pycroft on his first visit was that the list of occupants painted on the bottom of the wall of the passage did not include the 'Franco-Midland Hardware Company'. The premises inhabited by Pinner at the top of the lofty stair turned out to be 'a couple of empty and dusty little rooms uncarpeted and uncurtained'.

On their visit Holmes and Watson are introduced to Pinner as Mr Harris of Bermondsey and Mr Price of Birmingham, respectively, both looking for employment. Harris-Holmes identifies himself as 'an accountant'. This job description is singularly apt in its irony since we know Holmes is there to render accounts. And Watson is described as a 'clerk', which title is equally apt, since he is destined to dutifully record such accounting.

Soon after their arrival they have to save Mr Harry Pinner from hanging himself by his braces from a hook behind a door. Holmes is thereupon to reveal that Arthur and Harry Pinner are one and the same person. Pycroft comes to realise he has been the victim of an elaborate imposture, impersonated in London while engaged in Birmingham.

The attempt at suicide is the result of Pinner just having learned, from an early edition of the London *Evening Standard* Holmes observed Pinner buying in Corporation Street, that the ruse to tempt Pycroft from London had gone badly wrong. Pinner's real brother, a forger and safe-cracker, posing in a job Pycroft had hitherto been due to start, has been caught in the process of robbery, has murdered a watchman and looks doomed to hang.

Pycroft realises he has been fooled — illustration from *The Strand*.

The story of 'The Stockbroker's Clerk' judged by the exemplary standards Holmes set himself can hardly be deemed satisfactory. For had Holmes, instead of coming up to Birmingham, proceeded to the firm where Pinner's brother was posing as a clerk he might have saved the life of the unfortunate watchman and effected the capture of the fraudulent 'Mr Arthur Harry Pinner' in his own good time. In sum he would have saved one murder, one hanging and one attempted suicide.

Number 126 Corporation Street no longer exists. At the time Conan Doyle lived in Birmingham number 126 also does not appear to have

110

Holmes glances at the haggard Mr Pinner — illustration from *The Strand*.

existed, though the construction of Corporation Street, which was to radically transform the topography of central Birmingham, was well under way. By the time of the writing of 'The Adventure of the Stockbroker's Clerk' number 126 did exist, situated on the corner of Corporation Street and Lower Priory, opposite Old Square, which is the site, incidentally, where Dr Samuel Johnson began his literary career.[20] Lower Priory was done away with in the 1960s in the construction of Priory Ringway, finally abolishing number 126 Corporation Street altogether.

In the early 1890s 126 Corporation Street was occupied by a wholesale chemist, Magor Martin's 'Central Drug Stores', and also by the Central Wesleyan Chapel, Central Hall.[21] The Central Hall was to become known as King's Hall and leased for secular purposes, hosting vaudeville, cinema, billiards, and, later still, bingo, when the site of the old drug store was used as a café.[22]

Is it mere coincidence that Conan Doyle should have worked as a

126 Corporation Street, on the corner joining Priory Street, site of the offices of the 'Franco-Midland Hardware Company'.

drug dispenser in Birmingham and that the only story of his hero, Sherlock Holmes, actually set in Birmingham has its main action taking place in a part of Corporation Street which turns out to be occupied by a drug store? I cannot say positively whether it is coincidence or a little joke inspired by some experience with the Hoares. The case for the choice of 126 being deliberate is strengthened when we remember the use of the name of Horton the chemist's for Dr Hoare in *The Stark Munro Letters*.

There is another possible contribution to the choice of that part of Corporation Street for the Franco-Midland Hardware Company. Just a few yards along on the opposite side of the street was the County Court building, and next door to that Queen Victoria had in March 1887 laid the foundation stone for the imposing edifice of the new law courts which were to bear her name, and were opened in 1891, just a couple of years before the publication of 'The Adventure of the Stockbroker's Clerk.[23]

We know that Conan Doyle did return to Birmingham in December

112

Victoria Law Courts, Corporation Street.

1890 on his way back to the family home from Southsea.[24] It is not unreasonable to assume he visited Corporation Street by the tramway running directly from Aston Cross to New Street, witnessing as he did so the progress of work on Corporation Street and the law courts.

It is at the railway station in New Street that Holmes and Watson arrive — a station which has since been extensively rebuilt. And it is in New Street too that Pycroft stays at a hotel and does the business of Pinner's spurious company. Most likely Conan Doyle had in mind the present Midland Hotel, built to serve the trade of the nearby station in 1872, much renovated at the turn of the century for up-market purposes, and well placed for the landmarks of the city centre mentioned in the story, though there are several other possible options.

Next to 126 Corporation Street back in 1890 was the pit entrance to the New Grand Theatre, which it is quite possible Conan Doyle visited. He was familiar enough with places of local entertainment at that time to know of the attractions of Day's Music Hall, which the fraudulent company director Pinner commends to Pycroft as a break from his labours. Day's was a popular venue, handily situated for the

113

Midland Hotel, being just around the corner in Smallbrook Street. It provided a diversity of entertainment between 1862, when it was opened by James Day, till its closure in 1893.[25] Like the site of 126 Corporation Street, the site of Day's in Smallbrook Street has been swallowed up by a modern ring road, known now as Smallbrook Queensway.

Next to the New Grand Theatre pit entrance, and part of the same building as the theatre, at the time of Conan Doyle's return visit to the city was Edward Harris the tobacconist.[26] There was, as it happens, a cigar manufacturer James Harris near Clifton House in Aston Road North at the time Conan Doyle lived there. Harris is a common enough name to be sure — perhaps it is just too far fetched to suspect another of Conan Doyle's little jokes was his having Holmes make use of the name of 'Harris'. Although it will be remembered Conan Doyle was, like Sherlock Holmes and Dr Watson, and like Dr Hoare and his wife Amy, extremely fond of his tobacco.

With many of the Holmes tales where the dating of the action is not made quite explicit in the text it has become a little contentious: but we have the temerity to say that the year of the setting of 'The Adventure of the Stockbroker's Clerk' can be readily inferred. We are told that the adventure occurs three months after Dr Watson had taken up a practice started just after his marriage to Mary Morstan. Watson's marriage to Mary was the direct result of the adventures of *The Sign of Four*. Most critics concur on the grounds of internal evidence in that text that the action of *The Sign of Four* takes place in 1888, and the majority agree also that we can feel reasonably safe in ascribing the year 1889 for 'The Adventure of the Stockbroker's Clerk'.[27]

The year of 1889 has some significance for Birmingham civic history. Conan Doyle has Sherlock Holmes visiting Birmingham in the very year it celebrated its formal foundation as a city. What is more, he takes Holmes to a street which in its very construction, the brainchild of Joseph Chamberlain, symbolised the dynamism of the fast-emerging 'second city' of the British Empire. And it transpired that in the centenary year Sherlock Holmes duly returned to Birmingham; for November 13th of 1989 saw Jeremy Brett and Edward Hardwicke bring the play *The Secret of Sherlock Holmes*, a skilfully crafted homage to the detective written by Jeremy Paul, to the Alexandra Theatre, Birmingham after a successful West End run.

In the second Holmes story to feature Birmingham in a significant

114

way, 'The Adventure of the Three Garridebs', old Nathan Garrideb, a scholarly collector and recluse, is induced to take a day return ticket to Birmingham as the result of an elaborate tale told him by someone who identifies himself as John Garrideb from the USA.[28] The American claims they both will come into a lucrative inheritance if a third Garrideb can be located.

This time Holmes and Watson do not allow themselves to get diverted from the main scene of the action. They ensconce themselves in old Garrideb's flat off the Edgware Road in order to catch the miscreant in the act. This results in the capture of 'John Garrideb' alias 'Killer' Evans, who had been after the forgery equipment hidden under old Garrideb's floorboards by a criminal Evans has killed. The arrest of Evans furnishes another example of the great warmth Holmes feels towards Watson, who suffers a minor wound in the melée.

Meanwhile old Nathan has gone off to find Grosvenor Buildings in Aston — obviously this is supposed to be situated not far from Clifton House, Aston where Conan Doyle once lived and worked — as the result of a forged advert of one 'Howard Garrideb, Constructor of Agricultural Machinery'. Holmes is able to see through the falsity of the advert thanks to its tell-tale use of 'Americanisms'.

In both 'The Adventure of the Stockbroker's Clerk' and 'The Adventure of the Three Garridebs' Birmingham promises lucrative rewards but the promises prove chimerical. The city is used in order to get someone out of the way for a while for some misdoing to occur. Both stories involve forgery and misrepresentation. In fact both derive heavily in theme from the earlier somewhat more satisfactory story 'The Red-headed League.'[29] In this story there is also the deliberate diversion of a fabricated errand which is singularly offbeat; this time a pawnbroker is taken in so a crime can be prosecuted while the dupe is occupied elsewhere. Like 'The Adventure of the Three Garridebs' the futile mission is said to originate with a bizarre bequest of an eccentric American millionaire. Where the stockbroker's clerk of the later tale is stuck with copying out lists of hardware sellers from the *Paris Directory*, Jabez Wilson in 'The Red-headed League' is set to copy out the *Encyclopaedia Brittanica*. Again a notorious criminal's impersonation of a bona fide employee plays a crucial part in the intrigue. But 'The Red-headed League' has no such flaw as disappoints us in 'The Stockbroker's Clerk' — Holmes is on the spot to prevent the ruthless John Clay from getting away with duplicity. In this story access to the pawnbroker's cellar enables access also to the vaults of the adjoining bank.

It is tempting, but perhaps a mite unfair, to conclude that Conan Doyle is trying to tell us something or other about Birmingham in using it as the place of false hopes in 'The Adventure of the Stockbroker's Clerk' and 'The Adventure of the Three Garridebs'.

[1] A. Conan Doyle, 'The Five Orange Pips', *Strand*, November 1891 and *The Adventures of Sherlock Holmes*, (Newnes, 1892).

[2] James McGunn, *On Your Bicycle*, (John Murray, 1987), p. 65.

[3] Frederick Alderson, *Bicycling: A History*, (David and Charles, 1972), p. 38.

[4] Andrew Millward, 'The Cycle Industry in Birmingham 1890–1920' in Barbara Tilson (ed.) *Made In Birmingham*, (Brewin, 1989), pp. 165–178.

[5] Joan Skinner, 'Dunlop In Birmingham: The Making of an Industrial Empire', ibid., pp. 211–221.

[6] Millward, op. cit., p. 165.

[7] Harry How, 'A Day With Dr Conan Doyle', *Strand*, August 1892.

[8] A. Conan Doyle, 'The Adventure of the Solitary Cyclist', *Strand*, January 1904 and *The Return of Sherlock Holmes*, (Newnes, 1905).

[9] *Kelly's Directory for Warwickshire*, 1896–1904.

[10] A. Conan Doyle, 'The Adventure of the Three Gables', *Strand*, October 1926 and *The Casebook of Sherlock Holmes*, (John Murray, 1927).

[11] See Victor J. Price, *The Bull Ring Remembered*, (Brewin, 1989).

[12] A. Conan Doyle, 'Bendy's Sermon', *Strand*, April 1909 and in *Songs of the Road*, (Smith, Elder and Co, 1911).

[13] J. Dickson Carr, *The Life of Sir Arthur Conan Doyle*, (John Murray, 1949), p. 337.

[14] A. Conan Doyle, *Tales of the Ring and Camp*, (John Murray, 1922).

[15] A. Conan Doyle, *Rodney Stone*, (Smith, Elder and Co, 1896).

[16] A. Conan Doyle, *Memories and Adventures*, (Hodder and Stoughton, 1924), p. 276.

[17] A. Conan Doyle, 'The Adventure of the "Gloria Scott"', *Strand*, April 1893 and *The Memoirs of Sherlock Holmes*, (Newnes, 1893).

[18] A. E. Rodin and J. D. Key, *Medical Casebook of Dr Arthur Conan Doyle: From Practitioner to Sherlock Holmes and Beyond*, (Krieger, 1984), p. 243.

[19] A. Conan Doyle, 'The Adventure of the Stockbroker's Clerk', *Strand*, March 1893 and *The Memoirs of Sherlock Holmes*, (Newnes, 1893).

[20] *Kelly's Directory for Birmingham*, 1886–1892, and on the building of Corporation Street see Asa Briggs, *History of Birmingham* Volume 2, (Oxford University Press, 1952), pp. 19–21.

[21] *Kelly's Directory for Birmingham*, op. cit.

[22]Victor J. Price, *Birmingham's Theatres, Concert and Music Halls*, (Brewin, 1988), p. 34.

[23]Briggs, op. cit., pp. 21 – 22, pp. 88 – 89.

[24]Conan Doyle-Hoare Correspondence, letter no. 7 folio 3, 30.11.1890; letter no. 8 folio 3, 15.12.1890, Berg Collection, New York Public Library.

[25]Price, *Theatres,* op. cit., p. 29.

[26]*Kelly's Directory for Birmingham*, op. cit.

[27]Clues from the text have led Baring-Gould and others to conclude the exact date of the adventure can be put at Saturday 15th June 1889, but this has not gone unchallenged. See W. S. Baring-Gould, *The Annotated Sherlock Holmes* Volume II, (John Murray, 1968), p. 155.

[28]A. Conan Doyle, 'The Adventure of the Three Garridebs', *Strand*, January 1925 and *The Casebook of Sherlock Holmes*, (John Murray, 1927).

[29]A. Conan Doyle, 'The Red-headed League', *Strand*, August 1891 and *The Adventures of Sherlock Holmes*, (Newnes, 1892).

8

The Enduring Holmes

The stories of Sherlock Holmes show every sign of enduring popularity. But enduring memorials to Holmes and his creator in the Midlands of England are sparse. At the time of writing the Arthur Conan Doyle Society is in the process of getting a plaque erected in Ruyton-XI-Towns to commemorate Conan Doyle's four months there. And there is a plaque on 63 Aston Road North, Birmingham.... and a very minor mystery.

On the 29 October 1976 the present plaque was unveiled on the site of Dr Hoare's surgery, Clifton House. The ceremony was performed by Conan Doyle's youngest daughter, Dame Jean Conan-Doyle, Lady Bromet, in the presence of the actors then playing Holmes and Watson in the Birmingham Repertory Theatre's production of 'Sherlock Holmes'. This was to be the second plaque unveiled by Lady Bromet on the site in Aston; the first plaque, unveiled over twenty years earlier, had been of a less permanent nature than the neat blue cast iron Birmingham Civic Society plaque affixed there to this day, and had read, more modestly than its successor, 'Sir Arthur Conan Doyle Lived Here 1878 – 1879'.

There have been those who have commented, not without justice, that the present plaque in Aston Road North is rather misleading in recording that Conan Doyle lived there from 1878 to 1881. Aside from the question mark against the year Conan Doyle began at Clifton House, the plaque suggests his continuous residency. As we know, he was away from Dr Hoare's practice for periods lasting some months, on his adventures on a Greenland whaler in 1880, and around the West African coast from the autumn of 1881 till early 1882, when he came back to stay briefly at Dr Hoare's branch practice at 'The Elms', Erdington.

Plaque to Conan Doyle on 63 Aston Road North, Birmingham.

A Birmingham *Sunday Mercury* reporter in October 1976 told readers that the original hand-painted sheet metal plaque to Conan Doyle in Aston had been removed to the wall of the Thomas Startin's goods entrance. But it is no longer to be found anywhere on the site. The 1976 Birmingham Civic Society plaque on the front of the building is the only one now to be seen. In 1989, when researching the slim pamphlet *Sherlock Holmes In Birmingham*, the present author made enquiry at the site with the sales manager of Startin's who had worked at the place for the previous twenty-three years. Though the sales manager could recall well the 1976 ceremony which saw the unveiling of the new plaque he could not recall seeing the old plaque. He could not say where it had gone to but suggested I contact the Birmingham Civic Society. Enquiries at the said Society then drew a blank.

Back in October 1976 the *Mercury* reporter had asked 'What will become of the first plaque?' It appeared no-one knew or was saying in 1989. The trail has since gone colder. Thomas Startin's, a long-time neighbour dating from Victorian times, had taken over the site of Dr Hoare's house in the 1950s, vacated it late in 1989, and the place is, at the time of writing, advertised to let.

Another pertinent little matter which we may set beside 'The Case of the Missing Plaque' is 'The Adventure of the Baker Street Pillar Box'. Given that Baker Street in London is the locale more than any other to be associated with the great sleuth, as one could not but acknowledge at the outset of this book, a small architectural transplant has meant that a bit of that very street has now become a permanent part of the Midlands.

There is now to be seen, as part of the Black Country Museum near Dudley, Staffordshire, the original Penfold pillar box which had done duty in Baker Street at the time of the detective's fictional residency at 221B. The letter box had actually begun its existence as a Midlands product, having been manufactured by the Dudley firm of Cochrane, Grove and Company. It is what is known as a third variant Penfold box of a kind which was being produced, it is thought, from about 1872, almost ten years before Holmes and Watson's first adventure from their base in Baker Street. It would seem that our pillar box stood on the south-west corner of the junction of Baker Street and Blandford Street. The box was presented to the Borough of Dudley in September 1966 as a contribution to the regional museum collection representing industry and society in the area.

The mystery of the pillar box is related to what has been called 'The Riddle of Sherlock's Homes'. During the period of Holmes's fictional occupancy of Baker Street, from the beginning of the 1880s to 1903, there was no number 221B. Just exactly where in the street the detective was supposed to have been domiciled is a long running source of conjecture which in recent years has been further complicated by the presence of no less than two number 221 Baker Streets where once there were none.

Such secrets as the old Baker Street pillar box holds it is not giving away; and it is now located near the canal bridge in the Black Country Museum as part of a specially reconstructed Victorian village.

It is perhaps fitting that the story of 'Sherlock Holmes In The Midlands' should conclude with a couple of mysteries. Minutiae might often excite the great detective to remarkable efforts, though one dare not say that either 'The Case of the Missing Plaque' or 'The Adventure of the Baker Street Pillar Box' is worthy to be described by Sherlock Holmes as a 'three pipe problem'.

That Holmes can still be conjured up so readily, imagined engaged

The Baker Street pillar box in the Black Country Museum near Dudley.

in the solving of all manner of problems, is a tribute in itself to the extraordinary success Conan Doyle had in creating an illusion of reality. Something of the enduring power of Conan Doyle's creation is adduced too by the familiar and alluring notion that Holmes and Watson really existed. This invigorates the perennial quest, evidenced in the pages of this book, for authentic locations and individuals for the fictional adventures. The degree of plausibility which animates the tales was seen in relation to the Midlands as reinforced by reference to real life people and places; often a product of Conan Doyle's involvement in the area.

When Conan Doyle was tempted into playing Sherlock Holmes in 'real life' one found the outcome unconvincing. Unlike the Sherlock Holmes fiction, which is characterised by beginning with a teasing enigma the sleuth ultimately renders subject to reason, the unsolved and anomalous remained behind to haunt the legacy of the self-appointed detective after his supposedly conclusive discoveries had been made. Real life problems are inclined to be more complex and contradictory than the carefully structured contrivances of detective fiction.

But, notwithstanding Conan Doyle's limitations in the role of Sherlock Holmes, all credit must be due to one of the finest of story-tellers for having succeeded in creating a character who is an enduring inhabitant of everyone's imaginative landscape. The Midlands of England surely deserves to be acknowledged its part in the shaping of that character.

Acknowledgements

Acknowledgements are above all due to the outstanding contribution of Patricia Purchase to this work. She was responsible for taking over two dozen of the photographs featuring in this book. Acknowledgements for practical help must also go to Trevor Bailey, Hilary Morgan and Adrian de Redman. For material and assistance supplied me I must thank the Local Studies Department of the Birmingham Central Reference Library; the University of Birmingham; the Birmingham and Midland Institute; the Black Country Museum; the British Library; Cambridge University Library; Cannock Local Studies Department; Victor J. Price; R. and M. Whittington-Egan; the Berg Collection, New York Public Library; the Society for Psychical Research; the Public Records Office, Kew; the Sherlock Holmes Collection, Marylebone Public Library.